ABOUT THE AUTHOR

Rosie Sykes is a chef, writer and consultant. She has worked with some of the leading names in British food including Joyce Molyneux, Shaun Hill and Margot Henderson. She currently works as the development chef for Pint Shop in Cambridge and Oxford (pintshop.co.uk). She lives near Cambridge with her faithful hound Florence.

The Sunday Night Book

52 RECIPES TO MAKE
THE WEEKEND
FEEL LONGER

ROSIE SYKES

Photography by Patricia Niven

Hardie Grant

QUADRILLE

Publishing Director: Sarah Lavelle
Creative Director: Helen Lewis
Copy Editor: Alison Cowan
Designer: Will Webb
Photographer: Patricia Niven
Illustrator: Alexis Snell
Food Stylist: Rosie Reynolds
Prop Stylist: Rachel Vere
Production: Vincent Smith and Tom Moore

First published in 2017 by
Quadrille Publishing Limited
Pentagon House
52–54 Southwark Street
London SE1 1UN
quadrille.com

Quadrille is an imprint of Hardie Grant
hardiegrant.com

Cataloguing in Publication Data: a catalogue record for this book is available from the
British Library.

ISBN: 978 184949 965 1
Printed in China

Reprinted in 2020
10 9 8 7 6 5 4 3 2

CONTENTS

On toast 13

Onesies 27

A bowl of pasta 43

Excellent eggs 57

Spinach and goat's cheese soufflé omelette 58
Bombay potatoes and a fried egg 59
Eggs in a pestle and mortar 60
Baked mushrooms and eggs 61
Scrambled eggs with black pudding 62
Coddled egg Ivanhoe 63
Bacon and egg pie 65
Soft-boiled egg with asparagus soldiers 66
Mexican omelette 68

Comfort light 71

Watercress and beetroot salad with horseradish dressing
and a boiled egg 72
Satsuma, pomegranate, fennel and chicory salad
with feta 74
Quick soused mackerel with
bread-and-butter pickles 76
Smoked chicken, green bean and borlotti bean salad
with fig dressing 78
Jack's life-giving soup 80
A comforting bowl of dhal 81
Sam's salad: roast carrot and squash with orange,
pumpkin seeds and goat's cheese 83

Remains of the day 85

Chicken harira 86
Patatas bravas with a fried egg 88
Pork and cashew nut stir-fry 90
Bouillabaisse of peas and beans 92
Lamb and barley 93
Pizza by any other name 94
Epic bubble and squeak 96
Dripping on toast with chopped beef 97

Pick-me-ups and pop-it-in-in-ones 99

INTRODUCTION

When Ed Griffiths came to me with the idea for this book, it immediately evoked particular memories: the simple quick dishes we had as a family at home that were a welcome antidote to that Sunday night feeling. We were often all involved in an easy knock-together meal to be eaten on the sofa in front of the television, around a table with a game of cards or homework on the go, or with last-minute visitors. Wherever, whenever, whatever those Sunday night dishes involved, the memories are very warm.

As the weekend winds down into non-existence, many of us begin to contemplate the impending horrors that Monday morning will bring. But this is a choice, a social construct dictated by empty streets, empty pubs and closed curtains. You could resign yourself to yet another humdrum Sunday evening supper, but you could just as easily embrace the moment as an opportunity to create something that's not only comforting, but also uplifting.

This was my starting point, a desire to take up the Sunday night cause and come up with recipes that make it something to look forward to – a way to extend the joys of the weekend, if you will. From simple treats on toast, to eggs every which way, via some good housekeeping with leftovers or a light crisp salad, I hope I have made a collection of dishes that will delight. If all else fails just head straight for the cocktails in the pick-me-ups and pop-it-in-in-ones chapter.

On toast

For optimum comfort and speed, toast topped with
something easy and delicious is hard to beat.

Toast is the ultimate consolation on a Sunday night: crisp, yet soft and yielding. For me, it's always a winner, especially as it is so versatile. One of my best 'Toast Sundays' – and there have been many – was a big pile of toast plonked in the middle of the table with several treats to go on top and a load of friends and housemates coming and going. Late that evening was also when we came up with the 'Toast Office' cafe concept, which was pretty much based on that supper but with some clever tricks for keeping toast warm and crisp without it drying out. Watch this space, as they say...

I haven't specified what sort of bread to use in these recipes, as everyone will have their own favourites for toasting. And with so many of us wanting to eat less bread these days, I've also tried to make the toppings adaptable, so they'll sit just as happily on top of a bowl of steamed veg, rice, grains or even a piece of meat or fish.

CAERPHILLY WITH LEEKS
AND MUSTARD

This is a sort of less cheesy, more substantial Welsh rarebit. Leeks go splendidly with most cheeses, but are a particularly good match for the more citrussy flavours of something like Caerphilly. For those steering clear of bread, this would be super on cooked cauliflower or potatoes.

For 1
1 leek
1 tbsp light olive oil
2 sprigs of thyme
1 tbsp grain mustard
50g (½ cup) coarsely grated
  Caerphilly

1 thick slice bread of
  your choice
1 clove garlic, cut in half
sea salt and black pepper
ketchup or chutney, to serve

Trim the leek, keeping as much of the green top as possible, then wash well and cut into 2-cm (¾-in) slices. Put the olive oil into a large saucepan with a lid and place over a medium heat. Add the leeks, thyme and 2 tablespoons of water, stirring well to coat the leeks with the oily water. Season with a pinch of salt and a little pepper, then cover and cook for about 10 minutes, or until the leeks are very tender. Shake or stir the pan occasionally to stop them sticking, and add a little more water if the pan seems to be getting too dry before the leeks have softened.

Meanwhile, preheat the grill (broiler).

Once the leeks are soft and sweet, check they aren't sitting in too much liquid – they should glisten and just be coated. If there's too much liquid, remove the lid and let it simmer and reduce for a minute or so before stirring in the mustard and cheese. Lift out the thyme sprigs, then check the seasoning.

Toast the bread lightly on both sides and rub one side with the cut side of the garlic clove. Pile the cheesy leek mixture onto the toast and grill until the cheese is melting, bubbling and starting to brown.

Eat straight away with some ketchup or chutney, ideally homemade – the tomato sauce on page 88 goes really well.

DEVILLED CHICKEN LIVERS
ON TOAST WITH WATERCRESS

Devilled kidneys are definitely on the shortlist of things I would happily eat on a regular basis, but I know not everyone shares my taste for kidneys. Chicken livers done in the same manner are great, too, and I imagine have a wider appeal – just make sure you buy the very best chicken livers. They are quite rich and so a little devilling is a good foil.

For 3

300g (10½ oz) chicken livers
2 heaped tbsp plain
(all-purpose) flour
1 generous tsp English
mustard powder
¼ tsp cayenne pepper
2 tbsp sunflower or
rapeseed oil
2 tsp sherry vinegar

2 tsp Worcestershire sauce
100ml (generous ⅓ cup)
chicken or vegetable stock
30g (2 tbsp) butter
bunch of watercress
splash of extra virgin olive oil
2 tsp capers
sea salt and black pepper
3 thick slices toast of your
choice, to serve

Trim the livers of any sinew and discolouration. In a shallow dish, mix together the flour, mustard powder and cayenne. Season with salt and pepper and combine thoroughly. Dust the chicken livers with the flour, shaking off any excess and spreading them out on a plate.

Heat a large, heavy-based frying pan over a high heat, add the sunflower oil and, when hot, carefully add the chicken livers in a single layer. Once they are all in and sizzling nicely, turn the heat down a little to let them cook: you want a decent amount of heat to create a crisp devilish coat but not too much so that they char on the outside or become dry and rubbery inside. Turn the livers after a minute or so and cook on the other side for another minute, then lift them out onto a warm plate. Quickly splash the sherry vinegar and Worcestershire sauce into the frying pan and let them bubble away to almost nothing, then quickly pour in the chicken stock, stirring to deglaze the pan and capture all the flavours – I go at it with a whisk! Once the stock has reduced and thickened a little, swirl in the butter.
Return the livers to the pan for a moment or two just to warm them through.

Meanwhile, dress the watercress with the olive oil and capers and season with salt and pepper. Pile the watercress onto the warm toasts, divide the livers between them and strain the devilish liquor over the top.

ROAST FENNEL, CHICORY AND RED ONION WITH 'SILK WEAVER'S BRAIN'

Don't be put off by the mention of brain in the title: the Lyonnaise speciality of 'silk weaver's brain', or *cervelle de canut*, is actually a beautifully delicate herb-infused soft cheese, so named because silk weavers weren't considered to be that bright! I use Greek-style yoghurt to make the fresh cheese quickly and easily, but if you don't have the time or inclination to strain yoghurt, ricotta is a good substitute.

I absolutely adore roast fennel, finding it almost addictive. I always blanch it (and red onion) beforehand – it makes the roasting time shorter and ensures a sweet and tender result. Toast may seem like a cold-weather comfort but, as a massive toast fan, I'm always on the look-out for good summertime options, and this one fits the bill, I think. That said, it would work equally well without the toast, perhaps with some cooked green beans added to make it a little more substantial.

For 4	For the 'silk weaver's brain'
2 large heads of chicory (Belgian endive)	310g (11oz) Greek-style yoghurt
about 2 tbsp extra virgin olive oil	½ banana shallot
2 small fennel bulbs	4 sprigs of tarragon
1 red onion	small handful of flat-leaf parsley
juice of ½ orange	6 sprigs of mint
2 sprigs of basil	small handful of sorrel (optional)
sea salt and black pepper	3 lovage leaves (optional)
4 thick slices toast of your choice, to serve	1 tbsp extra virgin olive oil
	2 tsp red wine vinegar

Start with the fresh cheese – if you have time, it's a good idea to get this going in advance. Put the yoghurt into a fine sieve set over a bowl and leave to drain for a few hours, if possible, or just while you get everything else done.

Preheat the oven to 200°C/400°F/gas 6 with a large baking tray inside so that it heats up. Put a large pan of salted water on to boil.

Trim the chicory, discarding any bruised outer leaves. Take about four leaves from each head and set these aside for later, then quarter each head of chicory lengthwise and put in a bowl. Add a generous glug of olive oil, season with salt and pepper and toss to coat. Remove the hot baking tray from the oven, carefully tip in the chicory and return to the oven.

Now trim the fennel, cut in half lengthwise and then cut each half into three wedges. Peel the onion, cut in half and then cut each half into four wedges. Drop the fennel into the pan of boiling salted water and cook for a minute, then add the onion and cook for another 3 minutes, or until the vegetables yield slightly to the tip of a knife. Drain well, toss in some more olive oil and then add to the baking tray, giving the chicory a little shake at the same time. Return to the oven and leave everything to roast for 15–20 minutes, or until golden and sweet.

While the vegetables are roasting, finely chop the shallot and all the herbs for the 'silk weaver's brain'. Put them in a bowl with the olive oil and vinegar. Season with salt and pepper, then stir in the strained yoghurt, which should be quite firm by now, and amalgamate thoroughly. Check the seasoning and adjust if needed.

When the roast vegetables are ready, tip them into a large bowl and add the orange juice, along with some more salt and pepper and another splash of olive oil if necessary. Throw in the reserved raw chicory leaves, perhaps tearing any larger ones in half, then tear in the basil leaves and stir everything about.

Spoon the tasty juices from the bowl onto the toast and follow with the roast veg, then top with generous dollops of the 'silk weaver's brain'.

ANCHOVY TOAST WITH PARSLEY AND SHALLOT SALAD

Anchovy butter is a great fridge staple because it works with so many things: spread on toast to dip into a boiled egg, melted into pasta or rice with some spinach and olives, or rubbed over a lamb or pork chop with some lemon juice before grilling. And for a dairy-free version, just use 80ml (⅓ cup) light olive oil instead of the butter. A parsley and shallot salad always reminds me of the inspired accompaniment to roast bone marrow at the original St John restaurant in Smithfield, and of countless happy hours spent in the bar there since it opened.
Here is my slightly adapted version of Fergus Henderson's classic.

This supper sings warm summer evening to me, but if it doesn't feel substantial enough, a poached egg would be a good addition. And for non-toast-eaters, the salad and anchovy butter would work equally well slathered over some steamed purple sprouting broccoli or spinach or, for die-hard meat-heads, on a rare, grilled bavette steak.

For 2
1 small banana shallot,
   finely sliced
1½ tbsp olive oil
2 tsp sherry vinegar
1 tbsp capers
handful of flat-leaf parsley
1 little gem or ½ cos
   (romaine) lettuce, leaves
   separated
sea salt and black pepper
2 thick slices toast of your
   choice, to serve

For the anchovy butter
1 x 50g (2oz) tin of
   anchovies in olive oil
2 cloves garlic, roughly
   chopped
good pinch of chilli flakes
finely grated zest of
   1 lemon
150g (⅔ cup) butter
juice of 1 lemon

First, make the anchovy butter. Put the anchovies and the oil from the tin into a food processor, together with the garlic, chilli flakes and lemon zest, and whizz to a paste. If you're feeling energetic, a pestle and mortar will work too (and give you a little cardio workout as a bonus!). Melt the butter in a small saucepan and, with the motor running, pour it into the food processor in a slow steady stream to form a lovely emulsified paste. If using a pestle and mortar, slowly drizzle in the butter, mixing well to emulsify. Taste and add as much of the lemon juice as you think it can take. With the saltiness of the anchovies, I usually find the salt balance is good, but add a pinch if you think it needs it. The anchovy butter is ready to use, but it will last for several weeks in the fridge – I keep mine in a wide-mouthed jar and take it out of the fridge a good 20 minutes before I want to use it.

When you're ready to serve this marvellous supper, put the shallot into a bowl with the oil, vinegar and capers. Season with salt and pepper. Roughly chop the parsley and tear any larger lettuce leaves into smaller pieces. Add the parsley and lettuce to the bowl of shallot dressing and toss gently. Spread a good layer of anchovy butter onto hot toast and pile the salad on top.

TOMATOES WITH THYME AND BACON

During my time living in southern Spain, I developed a great love of *pan con tomate* (tomatoes squashed onto grilled bread). Although this is an Anglicized version, it still uses the tried-and-tested Spanish method of grating the tomatoes, which makes the whole prep thing much easier. These herby tomatoes go brilliantly with a fried egg, and would also work well with a bowl of pasta or rice instead of toast.

For 2

5 large plum tomatoes, halved
a generous splash of extra virgin olive oil
4 rashers of smoked streaky bacon

few sprigs of thyme – lemon thyme is extra nice with tomatoes
20g (1 tbsp) butter
sea salt and black pepper
2 thick slices toast of your choice, to serve

Working over a bowl to catch all the juices, grate the tomato halves on the coarse side of a grater, keeping hold of the skin – and being careful of your fingers! Discard the tomato skins.

Heat the oil in a frying pan over a medium heat. Using scissors, snip the bacon into chunky lardon-like pieces straight into the hot oil, then let it sizzle and release its fat. Once the bacon is cooked and a bit crispy, or however you like it, lift it out using a slotted spoon and set aside.

Add the grated tomato and thyme to the bacon fat in the pan, season with salt and pepper, and let it cook down to a lovely soft mass infused with the flavour of the thyme – this will take about 5–10 minutes at a good simmer. Add the butter and let it cook into the tomatoes for a minute, then return the bacon to the pan.
Fish out the thyme sprigs and spoon this deliciousness onto hot toast.

BUTTERY BLACK CABBAGE WITH CRUMBLED BLACK PUDDING

There is very little as good as steamy buttered greens. Black cabbage, or cavolo nero, has a strong constitution (which is why it is so important to cook it thoroughly in boiling salted water first) and works well with lashings of butter and a good dose of nutmeg. All of which goes hand in hand with crispy crumbled black pudding. If one were feeling particularly industrious, a poached egg on top would be a joy.

For 4

500g (1lb 2oz) black cabbage (cavolo nero)
6 spring onions (scallions)
about 3 tbsp light olive oil
2 cloves garlic, crushed
80g (⅓ cup) butter
grating of nutmeg

300g (10½oz) black pudding, thickly sliced
sea salt and black pepper
4 thick slices toast of your choice, to serve
mustard or pickle, to serve

Bring a pan of well-salted water to boil. Remove the tough stalks from the black cabbage and discard, then wash the leaves well. Add to the pan and cook until nice and soft, about 4–5 minutes – this makes the cabbage much more digestible. Drain the cabbage, rinse under cold water and squeeze dry.

Trim the spring onions and cut into 3-cm (1¼-in) lengths. Heat 2 tablespoons of the olive oil in a heavy-based saucepan over a medium heat and add the spring onions. Leave them to sizzle for a minute or so, then turn the heat down and let them stew for a few more minutes before adding the garlic. Let the garlic cook for a minute or so, then add the cabbage, along with the butter and a grating of nutmeg. When everything has warmed through and the butter has been absorbed into the cabbage, season with salt and pepper. Turn the heat right down and leave it ticking over very gently while you cook the black pudding.

Place a frying pan over high heat and add a splash of the olive oil. Crumble in the black pudding and cook, shaking the pan occasionally, until crispy.

Pile the buttery black cabbage onto toast and scatter over the black pud. Eat straight away, with mustard or pickle on the side.

LUCIO'S SARDINES

This recipe comes from a favourite kitchen porter I worked with at the Coach and Horses in Clerkenwell. He used to make it with fresh, scaled and gutted sardines cooked very, very slowly overnight with tomato, garlic, chilli, lemon, orange and coriander. By the morning, the sardines had disintegrated and we would smush them onto toast for our breakfast, lunch and dinner, or even just a snack because they were utterly delicious. I've doctored the recipe to make it quick and Sunday-night-able by using tinned sardines, which my sausage dog and I think are a very under-valued resource.

For 4

2 tbsp extra virgin olive oil
1 red onion, finely sliced
1 heaped tsp ground
   coriander seeds
1 heaped tsp ground
   fennel seeds
1 tsp chilli flakes
4 cloves garlic, finely sliced
200ml (generous ¾ cup)
   tomato juice
finely grated zest and
   juice of 1 orange

finely grated zest and
   juice of 1 lemon
small handful of flat-leaf
   parsley
large handful of coriander
   (cilantro)
3 x 120g (3¾oz) tins of
   sardines in olive oil
sea salt
4 thick slices toast of your
   choice, to serve

Heat the oil in a saucepan over a high heat. Add the onion, then turn the heat right down and let it cook without browning for a good 7 minutes. Once the onion is soft, add the spices and chilli flakes and cook, stirring, for a couple of minutes. Next add the garlic and let it cook for a minute before adding the tomato juice and the orange and lemon zests. Bring to a simmer and cook until reduced by half.

While that's happening, finely chop the parsley and coriander.

Open the tins of sardines and, keeping them whole, add the sardines and half of the oil from the tins to the pan. Stir gently to coat with the onion and spice mixture, then add the citrus juices and all but a generous pinch of each of the coriander and parsley. Let this lot simmer away gently until the juices have reduced right down to a syrupy coating, about 5–7 minutes.

Taste for seasoning, then spoon onto hot toast. Scatter over the remaining parsley and coriander.

BROWN SHRIMPS WITH WHISKY

Like many chefs, I love cooking at home for friends, but if I'm on my own I tend to make less effort, resorting mainly to toast and jam, or maybe a boiled egg. This little number is one I do make for myself, though, as it's so simple and pretty heavenly – all very uplifting if the Sunday-night blues are setting in…

For 1

1 x 57g (2oz) tub of potted shrimp
good pinch each of ground mace and cayenne pepper
2 tbsp whisky – as a peaty, malty type of girl, I
favour Islay
small clutch of chives
2 teaspoons crème fraîche
sea salt and black pepper
1 thick slice toast of your choice, to serve

Put the potted shrimp in a small saucepan and heat gently until the butter has melted. Turn up the heat and add the whisky, letting it bubble off almost entirely before adding the crème fraîche and snipping in the chives. When everything is warmed through, season with salt and pepper to taste and spoon onto toast.

ANCHOVY, CHILLI AND GARLIC
BEANS ON TOAST

Couldn't not have beans on toast in some guise. This recipe works with any beans really, but I like to use a small-ish bean for this, so cannellini or flageolet are my preference.

For 2
about 5 tbsp olive oil
2 x 50g (2oz) tins of
  anchovies in olive oil
1 red onion, finely sliced
1 large red chilli, deseeded
  and finely sliced
3 cloves garlic, crushed
finely grated zest and juice
  of 1 lemon

1 x 400g (14oz) tin of
  flageolet or cannellini
  beans
100g (3½oz) spinach leaves
small handful of flat-leaf
  parsley, finely chopped
2 thick slices toast of your
  choice, to serve

Heat 4 tablespoons olive oil in a saucepan over a low heat, add the anchovies and the oil from the tin and let them cook until melted down. Add the onion and cook gently for a good 15 minutes, stirring occasionally. Add the chilli, garlic and lemon zest and cook for a further couple of minutes.

Drain the beans, rinse them and add to the pan, then squeeze in the lemon juice and cook for 5 minutes to let everything get to know each other, stirring regularly. Finally, add the spinach and cook until just wilted.

Spoon the beans onto the toast, drizzle with olive oil, sprinkle the parsley on top and serve immediately.

Onesies

One-pot and one-baking-tray dishes – things that could carry over to a meal later in the week or go in a lunch box.

What's not to love about the one-pot plan? There's less washing up, for a start. At my sister's house of a Sunday evening, there's often something delicious bubbling away on the stove or baking in the oven. Anyone is welcome to come along and we often abandon the table mid-way through, with plates and napkins in hand, and head for the Sunday-night drama or a film...

SPICED RICE AND LENTILS

This makes a great accompaniment to a curry or a beautifully simple stand-alone supper, but can also become a speedy kedgeree with the addition of some flaked, smoked mackerel at the end. Alternatively, stir through some cooked vegetables and serve with yoghurt and herbs.

For 2

200g (1 cup) basmati rice
2½ tbsp sunflower or
  grapeseed oil
1 tsp brown mustard seeds
3 whole cloves
2 cardamom pods
1 large onion, finely sliced
5-cm (2-in) piece of fresh
  turmeric, peeled and finely
  grated, or 2 tsp ground
  turmeric
3 cloves garlic, crushed
2 red chillies, deseeded
  and finely chopped
2 tsp ground cumin

2 tsp ground coriander
100g (½ cup) red lentils,
  rinsed and drained
550ml (2¼ cups) chicken or
  vegetable stock
1 small cinnamon stick
1 bay leaf
2 eggs
3 spring onions (scallions)
generous handful of coriander
  (cilantro)
1 lime
40g (2 heaped tbsp) butter
sea salt
mango chutney or hot lime
  pickle, to serve

Rinse the rice well, then leave to soak until needed.

Heat 1½ tablespoons of the oil in a large heavy-based saucepan with a lid. Throw in the mustard seeds, cloves and cardamom pods and cook for a couple of minutes, until aromatic. Add the onion and soften down for 5–7 minutes, then turn up the heat to let it catch and brown a little before adding the turmeric. Stir for a minute to release its flavour and wonderful golden colour, then add the garlic, chillies, cumin and ground coriander. Give all the ingredients a couple more minutes of getting to know each other before adding the remaining tablespoon of oil.

When the oil is hot, add the lentils to the pan, stirring to coat with the onion and spice mixture. Drain the rice and add it to the pan as well, stirring to coat every grain before adding the stock, cinnamon stick and bay leaf. Season with salt, then bring to the boil and stir thoroughly. Clamp the lid on the pan and leave it over the lowest possible heat for 20 minutes.

Meanwhile, hard-boil the eggs, then peel and roughly chop. Trim and slice the spring onions, chop the coriander, and zest and juice the lime.

Once the rice and lentils are cooked, remove the pan from the heat and leave for 5 minutes before serving. Taste the rice and lentils for seasoning, then stir in the butter, lime zest and juice and coriander. Spoon into bowls and scatter with spring onions and chopped egg.

Serve with mango chutney or hot lime pickle.

CHERMOULA CHICKEN

Chermoula is a punchy North African spice paste that makes a great marinade for chicken, fish or vegetables. The chermoula itself can be made in advance, as it keeps well in the fridge for several days, then all you need to do for this super-simple one-pot meal is bung the chicken and vegetables in the oven and relax. Any leftovers will last for a couple of days in the fridge, and would make a great packed lunch shredded in a flatbread with some salad.

For 3, with some leftovers
10 chicken thighs, skin on
12 new potatoes, cut in half
  lengthways
2 red onions, cut in half and
  then into wedges
12 small tomatoes, cut in half
  – I like the little plum ones
sea salt

For the chermoula
1 tsp cumin seeds
½ lemon
decent handful of flat-leaf
  parsley, roughly chopped
decent handful of coriander
  (cilantro), roughly chopped
3 cloves garlic, crushed
½ red chilli, chopped –
  scrape out some of the seeds
  for less heat
1 tsp smoked paprika
6 tbsp light olive oil

For the chermoula, toast the cumin seeds for 1–2 minutes until aromatic, then leave to cool. Juice the lemon and finely chop the lemon husk you're left with. Run a knife through the cumin seeds a few times, just to break them up a bit and release their flavour. Put the parsley, coriander, garlic, chilli, smoked paprika, cumin and lemon juice into a food processor or large pestle and mortar. Add a teaspoon of the chopped lemon (reserve the rest for later) and ½ teaspoon of salt, then blitz or grind to a smooth, loose paste, slowly adding the olive oil to help the process.

Preheat the oven to 190°C/375°F/gas 5. Put the chicken thighs into a large roasting tin or baking dish and nestle the potatoes and onion wedges in between. Sprinkle with salt and scatter over the reserved chopped lemon. Add the chermoula and use your hands to rub it into the chicken and toss everything together. Make sure the chicken thighs are skin side up, then carefully pour in a cupful of water, trying not to wash the chermoula off the chicken and vegetables. Roast for about 30 minutes, then give everything a good stir and pour in a little more water if it seems too dry. Add the tomatoes and return to the oven for another 20 minutes.

After 50 minutes the chicken should be juicy with crisp, golden brown skin, and the potatoes cooked through. Everything else should have formed an unctuous sauce. If there doesn't seem to be enough sauce, transfer the chicken and vegetables to a warm serving dish, add some boiling water to the tin and scrape the bits from the bottom and sides – I find a whisk does this beautifully. Put the tin over a medium heat (or pour the sauce into a small pan if using a baking dish) and simmer the sauce for a minute or two, then pour over the chicken and serve straight away.

OLIVE, ANCHOVY AND ONION CORNBREAD TART

This hybrid of a savoury tarte tatin and a pizza uses cornbread instead of pastry or yeasted dough as its base, so it's a breeze to put together, quick to cook and very possible even on days when the fridge is looking stark and the store-cupboard is your only hope. One of the great joys of cornbread is that you can keep it simple or perk it up with some parmesan and spring onions. The best thing to make this tart in is a frying pan with a metal handle so you can put it in the oven.

For 4
4 red onions
1 tbsp balsamic vinegar
pinch of chilli flakes
2½ tbsp extra virgin olive oil
1 x 50g (2oz) tin of anchovies
3 tbsp marinated black olives, pitted
1 tbsp capers
sea salt and black pepper

For the cornbread
40g (⅓ cup) plain (all-purpose) flour
1¼ tsp baking powder
½ tsp bicarbonate of soda (baking soda)

150g (1 cup) fine polenta (cornmeal)
2 tsp soft brown sugar
½ tsp smoked paprika
2 eggs
120ml (½ cup) milk or plain yoghurt
15g (1 tbsp) butter, melted
45ml (3 tbsp) sunflower or grapeseed oil
35g (½ cup) freshly grated parmesan (optional)
2 spring onions (scallions), trimmed and finely sliced (optional)

Preheat the oven to 180°C/350°F/gas 4.

Peel the onions and cut them in half and then into wedges, letting the layers fall apart if they want to. Put the onions in a roasting tin or baking dish, add the balsamic vinegar, chilli flakes, 2 tablespoons olive oil and a generous pinch of salt and toss everything together. Cover with foil and cook for about 15 minutes until the onions are soft and sweet, stirring them a couple of times so they don't stick or burn and adding a few splashes of water if they start to look dry and crunchy. Remove the foil and return to the oven for another 5 minutes to let the onions absorb any liquid and brown a little.

Meanwhile, for the cornbread, sift the flour, baking powder and bicarbonate of soda together into a bowl, then stir in the polenta, sugar, paprika and ¾ teaspoon of salt. In another bowl, whisk together the eggs, milk or yoghurt, butter and oil – now is also the time to stir in the parmesan and spring onions, if using.

When the onions are done, remove them and turn the oven up to 200°C/400°F/ gas 6. Oil the base of a 20-cm (8-in) ovenproof frying pan or similar with the remaining ½ tablespoon olive oil. Arrange the anchovies in a diamond-shaped grid pattern all over the base of the pan, then place an olive in the centre of each diamond and scatter over the capers. Put the pan over a low heat, and when it is warm, cover the anchovies, olives and capers with a layer of onions, using a spoon to gently spread them out without disturbing the anchovies. Remove from the heat.

To finish the cornbread, add the wet ingredients to the dry and stir until just amalgamated – take care not to over-mix. Pour the batter into the hot pan and cook in the oven for 20 minutes or until a skewer or thin knife blade inserted into the centre comes out clean.

Leave the tart to rest for a few minutes before carefully inverting onto a serving plate. Serve warm.

SPICED BUTTER BEAN SOUP WITH FETA, AVOCADO AND TORTILLA CHIPS

This recipe comes from my sister Annabel, a very thorough and accomplished cook who brings loads of interesting things to my attention; this Latin American soup is no exception. It has become a firm favourite and definitely fits the Sunday-night bill.

For 2

1 tbsp extra virgin olive oil
1 large red onion, finely sliced
1 fennel bulb, trimmed and
    finely sliced
1 clove garlic, crushed
½ tsp ground cumin
1 tsp smoked paprika
pinch of cayenne pepper
1 x 400g (14oz) tin of butter
    beans, rinsed and drained
1 litre (4 cups) mixed vegetable

juice or tomato juice
100g (3½ cups) tortilla chips
100g (¾ cup) feta, crumbled
100g (¾ cup) stuffed olives,
    roughly chopped
1 avocado, chopped
generous handful of coriander
    (cilantro), roughly chopped
finely grated zest and juice
    of 1 lime
sea salt

Heat the oil in a large heavy-based saucepan with a lid. Add the onion, along with a pinch of salt, then put the lid on the pan and let the onion soften over a low heat for about 7 minutes. Add the fennel and, when that has softened, add the garlic. Turn the heat up to medium–high and add the spices, stirring them while they toast for a minute or so. Add the beans and vegetable juice, give everything a good stir, then put the lid back on and leave to simmer for 10 minutes.

Put the grill (broiler) on a low setting. Spread out half of the tortilla chips on a large baking tray and pop under the grill until they are hot. Drop the rest of the tortillas into the pan of beans and leave them to disintegrate and thicken the soup.

Meanwhile, mix together the feta, olives, avocado, coriander and lime zest.

Taste the soup for seasoning and add the lime juice. To serve, spoon into warm bowls and top with the feta mixture and the toasty tortilla chips.

WATERCRESS POTATOES
WITH PRAWNS

Watercress has a wonderful peppery flavour that goes really well with fish. In this quick supper dish, I sometimes leave out the prawns and just serve the potatoes in watercress sauce alongside a nice piece of grilled or roasted fish.

For 3

600g (1lb 5oz) floury potatoes, such as King Edward
120g (4 cups) watercress
splash of sunflower or grapeseed oil
150ml (scant ⅔ cup) milk
100ml (generous ⅓ cup) crème fraîche

250g (9oz) cooked and peeled North Atlantic, prawn-cocktail-type prawns (shrimp)
5 spring onions (scallions)
1 tsp creamed horseradish (optional)
squeeze of lemon juice
sea salt and black pepper

Preheat the oven to 180°C/350°F/gas 4.

Start by peeling the potatoes and cutting them into slices about 3mm (⅛ in) thick. Put the potato slices into a large saucepan of salted water and bring to the boil, then simmer for about 5–8 minutes or until they yield to the tip of a knife.

Meanwhile, put a generous splash of oil in a saucepan with a lid that will hold all the watercress. Place over a medium heat, add the watercress and toss until it starts to wilt, then cover with the lid and leave for a minute so the stalks soften down. Pour in the milk and bring to a simmer, then remove from the heat and stir in the crème fraîche. Tip the whole lot into an upright blender (or use a stick blender in the pan) and whizz to a green-flecked sauce.

When the potatoes are ready, drain then return to the pan and pour in the watercress sauce. Gently toss together and season with salt and pepper. Spoon half of the potatoes into a baking dish that will fit them all snugly, spreading them out evenly.

Mix together the prawns, spring onions, horseradish and lemon juice and spoon over the potatoes in the baking dish. Cover with the rest of the potatoes, pouring over any remaining watercress sauce in the pan.

Place on a baking tray and cook in the oven for about 25–30 minutes, or until the potatoes are completely cooked and a knife goes easily through them. Serve straight away.

TOMATO, SQUASH AND CREAMED KALE GRATIN

In a way, this is like a pasta-free lasagne: a tomato, red pepper and sweetcorn sauce is layered with thin sheets of squash, and creamed kale acts as the bechamel sauce. I wrote the original version of this recipe for an amazing charity called Farm Africa which, among many other things, helps children to grow vegetables in their schoolyards, so I chose vegetables they might be likely to grow successfully. The project means they get at least one nutritious meal a day, and any surplus can be sold commercially, benefiting the whole community.

For 4
400g (14oz) squash
400g (14oz) kale
1 tbsp extra virgin olive oil
finely grated zest and juice
    of 1 lemon
small pinch of chilli flakes
15g (1 tbsp) butter
80ml (⅓ cup) double
    (heavy) cream
80g (⅓ cup) cream cheese
50g (1 cup) panko or other
    breadcrumbs
1 tbsp pumpkin seeds, roughly
    chopped
20g (⅓ cup) freshly grated
    parmesan
sea salt and black pepper

For the tomato sauce
3 tbsp extra virgin olive oil
1 medium onion, finely sliced
1 small red (bell) pepper,
    deseeded and sliced
2 cloves garlic, crushed
1 x 200g (7oz) tin of
    sweetcorn, drained
1 x 400g (14oz) tin of peeled
    chopped tomatoes
1 large bay leaf
generous sprig of rosemary

Preheat the oven to 180°C/350°F/gas 4.

Start by making the tomato sauce. Heat 2 tablespoons of the oil in a heavy-based saucepan, add the onion and a pinch of salt and cook for 7 minutes, stirring occasionally, until softened. Add another tablespoon of oil and the red pepper and cook for 5 minutes, stirring occasionally, until tender. Add the garlic and cook for a minute before stirring in the sweetcorn, tomatoes, bay leaf and rosemary. Season well with salt and pepper, then bring to a simmer and cook for 15 minutes, stirring occasionally, to make a nice rich sauce. Fish out the bay leaf and rosemary and check the seasoning.

While the sauce is cooking away, bring a large saucepan of salted water to the boil. Peel and deseed the squash, then cut into slices about 3mm (⅛ in) thick, keeping in mind that you'll be using them like sheets of pasta in a lasagne. Remove the tough stalks from the kale, wash well and chop roughly. Blanch the squash slices in the boiling water for a minute or two, until just tender, then carefully lift out and leave to drain. Blanch the kale for a bit longer, for about 5 minutes, so it's thoroughly wilted and has lost any hint of squeakiness. Drain and refresh under cold running water to prevent it cooking further, then use your hands to squeeze out as much excess moisture as possible.

Drizzle the squash with the oil and lemon juice, then sprinkle over the lemon zest and chilli flakes and season with salt.

Melt the butter in a frying pan over a medium heat and add the kale. Season with pepper and sauté for a couple of minutes until heated through. Stir in the cream and allow to bubble down and reduce until the cream is coating the kale nicely, then add in the cream cheese and mix thoroughly. Check the seasoning.

Mix together the breadcrumbs, pumpkin seeds and parmesan.

Spoon half of the tomato sauce into a large baking dish. Top with half of the squash slices, then cover with half of the creamed kale. Repeat these three layers, then scatter over the breadcrumb mixture. Bake for 30 minutes, or until the topping is crisp and the vegetables are piping hot.

JERUSALEM ARTICHOKE, HAZELNUT AND GOAT'S CHEESE TART

Filo tarts are deceptively simple to make and so delicious. Once you've got the technique right you can put whatever you like on top – this combination is a particular favourite of mine, though, especially when served with a salad of bitter leaves and orange segments. The thyme-infused oil keeps well for at least a month, strained into a clean and dry jar or bottle and stored in a cool, dark place, so you might want to make double the amount. You'll soon find countless uses for it: try it in salad dressings, or drizzled over roast veg or a nice piece of fish or meat.

For 4
6 tbsp light olive oil	juice of ½ lemon
2 cloves garlic, lightly squashed with the back of a knife	250g (9oz) Jerusalem artichokes
zest of ½ lemon, peeled off in strips	200g (7½oz) filo pastry, thawed if frozen
4 sprigs of thyme	60g (2oz) soft goat's cheese
40g (⅓ cup) hazelnuts	sea salt and black pepper
2 leeks	

Start by making the infused oil. Put 4½ tablespoons olive oil in a small heavy-based saucepan over the lowest possible heat and add the garlic, lemon zest and two of the thyme sprigs. Let it warm gently and infuse for about 10 minutes. Don't let the oil overheat or the flavourings will burn – if it starts to bubble or smoke, quickly take it off the heat. Once the oil has infused, cover the pan tightly with cling film (this will intensify the flavour of the oil as it cools) and set aside until needed.

Preheat the oven to 200°C/400°F/gas 6 and put a baking sheet in to heat at the same time. While the oven is heating up, spread the hazelnuts out on a baking tray and put in to toast for a couple of minutes. Their high fat content means they burn easily, so keep an eye on them. As soon as they turn light golden and their skins come away easily, remove from the oven. While they are still warm, wrap in a clean tea towel or some kitchen paper and give them a rub – this will encourage the skins to come off. Lift out the now mostly skinless nuts and leave to cool.

Meanwhile, wash, trim and thinly slice the leeks. Heat the remaining 1½ tablespoons oil in a saucepan with a lid and add the leeks, together with the leaves stripped from the remaining two thyme sprigs. Put the lid on and leave the leeks to cook over a low heat for about 10 minutes or until meltingly soft – turn the heat down if they start to brown. Squeeze in the lemon juice (reserving the empty lemon half), then turn up the heat to evaporate any excess liquid. When the leeks are pretty dry, season them with salt and pepper, then take off the heat and set aside.

While the leeks are cooking, scrub the artichokes and slice them into rounds as finely as you can, dropping them straight into a bowl of water with the lemon husk or some vinegar added to stop them from discolouring.

Strain the thyme-infused oil, which will have a wonderful scent, and chop the cooled hazelnuts quite finely.

To assemble the tart, brush a large baking tray, about 40cm x 30cm (16in x 12in), with infused oil. Place a layer of filo pastry on the baking tray: the tart should be around 25cm (10in) square – you may need two sheets of filo, placed side by side with some overlap, to achieve this. Brush this first layer with oil and scatter with a fifth of the hazelnuts. Put the next layer of filo on top, pressing down well, then repeat the oil brushing and hazelnut scattering. Add two more layers of pastry, oil and nuts, finishing with a final layer of pastry.

Now for the toppings. Cover the pastry base with an even layer of soft leeks, then carefully arrange the artichokes on top in slightly overlapping rows. Brush with a little infused oil, if there is any left; if not, a drizzle of olive oil will do. Season with salt and pepper and crumble over the goat's cheese, then put the baking tray straight onto the hot baking sheet in the oven and bake for about 20–25 minutes, or until the pastry base is crisp and brown and the goat's cheese has melted and is flecked with golden spots. Cut the tart into four and dive in.

HAM AND MACARONI SOUP

Soup makes a warming Sunday-night supper, and this broth is a lovely lighter option. I tend to cook this one around Christmas, when there's usually ham and often the requisite ham bone to make a good stock – and a lighter meal is generally very welcome! If your fridge is groaning with leftovers, feel free to add a bit of turkey or goose, and some sprouts or other greens instead of the spinach.

For 2

1 tbsp light olive oil
1 small red onion, finely sliced
1 leek, washed, trimmed
   and thinly sliced
1 stick of celery, washed and
   diced
1 carrot, peeled, halved
   lengthways and then sliced
2 cloves garlic, finely sliced
couple of sprigs each of
   thyme and sage
1 bay leaf
strip of lemon zest

500ml (2 cups) ham or
   vegetable stock
200g (7oz) cooked ham,
   shredded
2 handfuls of baby spinach,
   well washed
100g (¾ cup) macaroni
generous handful of flat-leaf
   parsley, chopped
sea salt and black pepper
freshly grated parmesan,
   to serve

Heat the oil in a large heavy-based saucepan, add the onion, together with a pinch of salt, and soften over a low heat for about 7 minutes, stirring occasionally. Turn the heat up to high, add the leek, celery and carrot to the pan and cook for 5 minutes, stirring often. Add the garlic, along with the herbs and lemon zest and stir about for a couple of minutes, then pour in the stock and season lightly with salt and pepper. Bring the broth to a simmer, reduce the heat and cook gently for about 20 minutes.

Meanwhile, cook the macaroni in plenty of boiling salted water until nicely *al dente*.

After the broth has been cooking for 20 minutes, add the ham, spinach, macaroni and parsley and leave them to warm through in the hot broth. This will take about 5 minutes, so turn the heat right down, as you don't want the ham to boil and become dry and tough. Check the seasoning, then serve in big warm bowls with parmesan grated on top.

A bowl of pasta

Makeovers for the classic store-cupboard staple.

There has been a steep increase in pasta eating since my youth. Back then, we might have had macaroni cheese, spag bol or lasagne, but nothing more adventurous. Then, in the late 1980s, pasta of every shape and size became the thing to have, and so it has continued. As a bowl of pasta makes such a quick, easy and filling meal, this is totally understandable. Plus, the possibilities are endless: I think everyone has a pasta dish they consider their own. My mum's was macaroni cauliflower cheese with some ham or bacon thrown in, if we were very lucky.

FREGOLA WITH BACON AND PEAS

Fregola is a bobbly Sardinian pasta that I really like, partly due to my deep love of the texture of sago and tapioca. Cooking it with peas makes for a pleasingly spherical supper. This is a sort of soupy dish, a bit like *risi e bisi*.

For 2

150g (1 cup) fregola
100g (¾ cup) frozen peas
1½ tbsp light olive oil
60g (2oz) smoked streaky
  bacon
1 banana shallot, finely sliced
100ml (generous ⅓ cup)
  white wine

400ml chicken or
  vegetable stock
30g (2 tbsp) butter
30g (⅓ cup) freshly grated
  parmesan
3 sprigs mint, leaves picked
  and finely chopped
sea salt and black pepper

Bring a large pan of salted water to the boil and cook the fregola for half its cooking time, about 8 minutes, adding the peas for the last 2 minutes. Drain and rinse under cold running water, then set aside.

Heat the oil in a heavy-based saucepan over a medium heat. If your bacon has the rind still on, remove and reserve. Using scissors, snip the bacon into 1-cm (½-in) pieces directly into the hot oil – adding any reserved rind for extra flavour – then let it sizzle and give off its fat. Once the bacon is cooked and a bit crispy, lift out with a slotted spoon and set aside; discard the rinds or give them to the birds.

Add the shallot to the residual fat in the pan and cook over a low heat for about 5 minutes, or until soft, stirring so it doesn't catch too much colour. Stir in the fregola and peas, then pour in the white wine. Once the wine has evaporated, add the stock. Bring to a simmer and cook until the fregola is just cooked, about another 6 minutes.

Return the bacon to the pan, then add the butter and all but a tablespoon of both the parmesan and the mint. Stir over a low heat for a couple of minutes, then cover and remove from the heat. Let it sit for another minute before spooning into bowls. Scatter over the remaining parmesan and mint, then inhale – this is super-delicious!

MACARONI CAULIFLOWER CHEESE

Very comforting on a cold night, this version of mac and cheese is made lighter by the inclusion of cauliflower, and the breadcrumb topping adds some much-needed texture. When I was a kid, my mum used crumbled-up Weetabix for this, which was quite lovely, if a little kooky in retrospect – I guess the modern version is the panko breadcrumb. Feel free to try them all out and settle on your own mix. I like to serve this with some rocket or other peppery salad leaves.

For 3–4, depending on hunger levels
500ml (2 cups) milk
1 bay leaf
1 tsp black peppercorns
pinch of nutmeg
200g (7oz) macaroni
1 good-sized cauliflower, about 750g (1lb 10oz), broken into small florets
40g (2 heaped tbsp) butter
4 spring onions (scallions), trimmed and sliced, including green parts
40g (⅓ cup) plain (all-purpose) flour
2 tsp English mustard
pinch of cayenne pepper or chilli powder
120g (1⅓ cups) grated cheddar
50g (1 cup) stale bread, chopped into small pieces
generous sprig of thyme, leaves picked, or ½ tsp good-quality dried thyme
30g (⅓ cup) freshly grated parmesan
sea salt and black pepper

Preheat the oven to 200°C/400°F/gas 6. Put a large saucepan of salted water on to boil.

In another saucepan, warm the milk over a low heat with the bay leaf, peppercorns and nutmeg. Once the milk reaches simmering point, remove from the heat and cover the pan, then leave to infuse while you cook the macaroni. If you are in a mad rush, you can leave this step out – it just adds another dimension of comfort and warmth to the dish. Either way, it's a good idea to quickly warm the milk before making the white sauce.

When the water is boiling, add the macaroni and cook for 8 minutes or as instructed on the packet, adding the cauliflower halfway through the cooking time. When they are both tender, drain well and tip into a large baking dish. Season lightly with salt and pepper and give it all a stir.

continued overleaf

While the macaroni is cooking, make the white sauce. Melt the butter in a small saucepan, then add the spring onions and cook for a couple of minutes. Add the flour and stir to make a thick paste, cooking the flour out for a minute or so until it smells biscuity and has a very light brown tinge. Stir in the mustard and cayenne, then gradually add the warm milk, pouring it through a sieve to catch the infusion ingredients, and stirring well between each addition. Cook, stirring constantly, over a medium heat until you have a smooth sauce that coats the back of the wooden spoon. Add the grated cheddar and stir until it has melted, then check for seasoning. Pour the sauce over the macaroni and cauliflower in the baking dish.

Mix the roughly chopped bread with the thyme and parmesan, then scatter over the top. Bake the macaroni cheese for about 15 minutes or until bubbling and golden brown.

TOASTED SPAGHETTI WITH RED ONIONS, ALMONDS AND RAISINS

Toasting pasta gives it a wonderfully nutty flavour. The trickiest part of this recipe is herding the toasted spaghetti into the boiling water. Because it's slippery, tongs don't work, so it's just a case of gentle guidance and persistence – experience of which has led me to make the controversial suggestion of snapping it in half pre-toasting!

I have gone for a Sicilian-inspired sweet and sour vibe to the sauce, and included wild garlic since the toasty pasta makes a perfect foil for it. Wild garlic grows in woodland and is only in season for a few weeks in late spring, but it is a most excellent treat and these days canny foragers have made it easier to buy. When wild garlic is out of season or unavailable, just use a couple of finely sliced cloves of garlic and a handful of chopped parsley instead.

For 4

400g (14oz) spaghetti,
    snapped in half
3 tbsp extra virgin olive oil
20g (1½ tbsp) butter
3 large red onions, finely sliced
40g (¼ cup) raisins
40g (⅓ cup) blanched
    almonds
1 tbsp white wine vinegar

100ml (generous ⅓ cup)
    white wine or dry cider
200g (7oz) wild garlic,
    washed, trimmed and
    roughly shredded
sea salt and black pepper
40g (⅔ cup) freshly grated
    parmesan, to serve

Preheat the oven to 170°C/325°F/gas 3.

Put the spaghetti onto a large baking tray, sprinkle with 1 tablespoon of the olive oil and rub thoroughly into the pasta. Spread the strands out into an even layer, then toast in the oven for 7 minutes. Give the tray a good shake and turn it around, then return it to the oven for another 5 minutes. By now the spaghetti should be a rich golden brown, with the tips maybe a little darker. Give it a little longer if you think it needs it, but keep checking often, as it will burn very quickly.

While the pasta is in the oven, put the rest of the olive oil and the butter in a heavy-based saucepan with a lid, add the onions and bring them up to a sizzle over a high heat. Add a pinch of salt, pop the lid on and turn the heat right down.

continued overleaf

Leave the onions to soften for a good 15 minutes, stirring from time to time to avoid them browning too much or sticking.

Soak the raisins in boiling water for about 10 minutes. Toast the almonds in the oven for 5 minutes, then roughly chop. Once the onions are meltingly soft, take the lid off, turn the heat right up and add the vinegar and wine. Bring to the boil, then reduce the heat and leave to simmer until the liquid has pretty much evaporated. Now throw in the wild garlic, put the lid on again and let it wilt down for a few minutes. Stir in the drained raisins and season with salt and pepper.

Bring a very large pan of salted water to the boil. Carefully add the toasted spaghetti and cook for 7–10 minutes, depending on how you like your pasta – bear in mind that it will be drier post-toasting and so will take a little longer to cook. Drain and return to the pan, then tip in the onion-garlic mixture and stir thoroughly. Check the seasoning and stir in the almonds.

Pile the spaghetti onto warm plates and serve with grated parmesan – I tend to scatter a little on top and then let people add more to taste.

CAERPHILLY WITH LEEKS AND MUSTARD

(see page 14)

TOMATOES WITH THYME AND BACON

(see page 20)

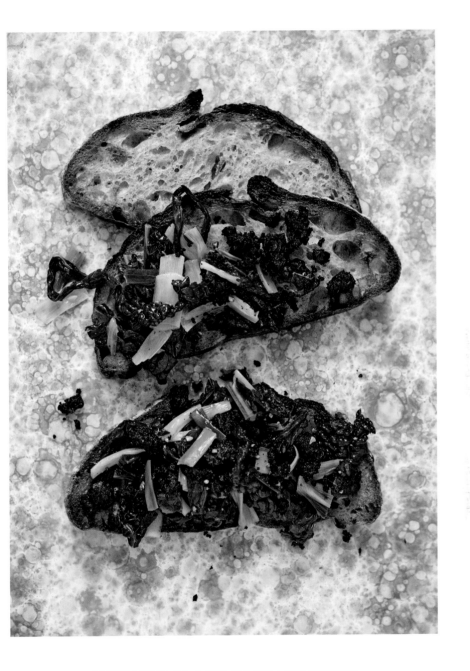

BUTTERY BLACK CABBAGE WITH
CRUMBLED BLACK PUDDING

(see page 21)

CHERMOULA CHICKEN

(see page 30)

JERUSALEM ARTICHOKE, HAZELNUT
AND GOAT'S CHEESE TART

(see page 38)

TOMATO, SQUASH AND
CREAMED KALE GRATIN

(see page 36)

HAM AND MACARONI SOUP

(see page 40)

FREGOLA WITH BACON AND PEAS

(see page 44)

MACARONADE

What's not to love here? Macaroni – already a favourite in most households – mixed with delicious stock (or gravy) and cheese, so you get all the benefits of macaroni cheese but without the heaviness of a white sauce, plus it's a great way of using up the gravy from Sunday lunch. If there's any leftover meat, you could have it alongside too, but I find this a wonderfully comforting Sunday-night treat all on its own.

I introduced my great friend and co-author of *The Kitchen Revolution*, Polly Russell, to macaronade and she absolutely raved about it. Apparently the whole family loves it – no easy feat when catering for children! So now, whenever she makes a casserole, she always makes a bit of extra gravy or sauce, then she can knock this up at the drop of a hat.

For 2
180g (1½ cups) macaroni
600ml (2⅓ cups) stock or
  gravy – beef, chicken or
  even ham – or leftover
  sauce from a stew
2 bay leaves
few sprigs each of rosemary
  and thyme

small handful of flat-leaf
  parsley, chopped
30g (½ cup) freshly grated
  parmesan
30g (½ cup) panko or
  other breadcrumbs
  – I like soft-ish ones
sea salt and black pepper

Bring a large saucepan of salted water to the boil and cook the macaroni until *al dente*.

Meanwhile, pour the stock into another pan and add the bay leaves, rosemary and thyme. Bring to the boil and simmer until reduced by a third.

Preheat the grill (broiler) to high.

Drain the macaroni well. Tip half of it into a baking dish and strain over half the reduced stock, then stir in half the parsley. Scatter over half the parmesan and cover with the rest of the macaroni. Mix the breadcrumbs with the remaining parmesan and parsley, then pour the rest of the reduced stock over the macaroni and scatter over the cheesy crumbs.

Pop the macaronade under the grill until bubbling, golden brown and crisp.

RICHARD'S CRAB LINGUINE

My brother-in-law Richard is a very competent cook and this is something that regularly appears at his house. I absolutely love it and would almost certainly have it on my desert-island-dish list. The original recipe comes from the wondrous Laura Santtini's book *Easy Tasty Italian* – but, like all these sorts of things, Richard now has his own version, and I have a version of his version! I use a dressed crab, if I can find one, and an average one of those is ample for three people. Otherwise, I use a tiny bit more white meat than brown.

For 3

270g (9½oz) linguine
1 small whole dressed crab, or 120g (4oz) brown and 150g (5½oz) white meat
2 garlic cloves, roughly chopped
small handful of flat-leaf parsley, roughly chopped

1 tsp chilli flakes
finely grated zest and juice of 1 lemon
100ml (generous ⅓ cup) extra virgin olive oil
sea salt

Bring a large saucepan of salted water to the boil, add the linguine and cook as instructed on the packet – depending on the brand, the suggested cooking time can vary from 8–12 minutes.

While the pasta is cooking, put the garlic, parsley, chilli flakes and lemon zest into an upright blender or the goblet of a stick blender. Add a couple of tablespoons of the olive oil and blend to a paste. Add a good pinch of salt and the rest of the olive oil, along with half of the lemon juice, and briefly blend again.

Check through the crab for any tiny shards of shell, then put the meat into a bowl. Pour in the mixture from the blender and stir well. Check the seasoning and add more lemon juice, chilli or salt as you feel inclined.

Once the pasta is ready, drain well and return to the pan. Stir in the crab mixture thoroughly, then serve immediately, perhaps passing around some extra lemon for squeezing on top if you haven't already used all the juice.

CATALAN ANGEL-HAIR PASTA
WITH SEAFOOD

This is based on the Catalan dish called *fideua*, which I finally got around to making about six months ago, having been fascinated by it for years. Essentially it's along the lines of paella, but made with thin spaghetti-like pasta, and it was definitely worth the wait. The prawns you're after for this are the ones still in their shells that you get in a pint glass at proper pubs and by the sea. Try to buy them from a fishmonger, then you can pick up the mussels, haddock and some extra bones for the stock at the same time – the extra flavour from the fish bones will make all the difference to the finished dish. A good aioli goes nicely with *fideua*, but isn't obligatory, and all it really needs is a simple green salad.

For 4
600g (1lb 5oz) haddock on
    the bone, plus a few extra
    bones if possible
100g (3½oz) smoked haddock
500g (1lb 2oz) angel-hair
    pasta
3 tbsp extra virgin olive oil
pinch of saffron strands,
    soaked in 100ml (scant
    ⅔ cup) warm water
500g (1lb 2oz) mussels,
    scrubbed and debearded
finely grated zest and juice
    of ½ lemon
1 clove garlic, finely grated
generous handful of flat-leaf
    parsley, finely chopped
sea salt and black pepper

For the stock
2 tbsp light olive oil
2 red onions, roughly chopped
200g (7oz) shell-on North
    Atlantic prawns (shrimp)
4 cloves garlic, lightly squashed
    with the back of a knife
1 tsp cayenne pepper
1 tsp smoked paprika
½ tsp fennel seeds
1 bay leaf
few sprigs of thyme
5 black peppercorns
juice and zest of ½ orange,
    peeled off in strips
150ml (scant ⅔ cup)
    white wine
150ml (scant ⅔ cup)
    tomato juice
1 litre (4 cups) water

Take the haddock off the bone and save that for the stock, then cut both the fresh and smoked fish into bite-sized chunks and set aside.

For the stock, heat the light olive oil in a stockpot or large saucepan over a medium heat. Add the onions and cook until golden brown, then add any fish bones and the prawns.

continued overleaf

Let these cook for a minute or so before adding the garlic, cayenne, paprika, fennel seeds, peppercorns, bay leaf, thyme and orange zest. Stir for a moment until aromatic, then add the orange juice, white wine, tomato juice and water. Bring to the boil, then turn down the heat and leave to simmer for 30 minutes. Pour the stock through a fine sieve into a jug, pressing down with the back of a spoon or ladle to get all the oils and flavours out.

When you're ready to make the *fideua*, heat a paella pan, or heavy-based frying pan over high heat and add 2 tablespoons of the extra virgin olive oil. Break the angel-hair pasta into shorter lengths and add to the pan. Cook, stirring constantly, for 5 minutes or until the pasta has taken on some colour. Now add 600ml (2½ cups) of the warm stock and bring to a simmer, using a wooden spoon to make sure all the pasta is immersed in the stock. Let it cook for a few minutes, then add the saffron and its soaking water. Give everything a good stir then pour in enough stock to cover the pasta by about 2cm (¾in). Simmer for another 7 minutes, adding more stock if it starts to look too dry. Add the mussels, making sure they are well immersed, and adding a little more stock if necessary. Now leave the whole lot to bubble away until the mussels open.

While that is happening, heat the remaining tablespoon of extra virgin olive oil in a frying pan or large saucepan. Season the fish with salt and pepper and fry until it is just cooked, for about 5 minutes, depending on the size of the chunks. Squeeze in the lemon juice and scatter over the lemon zest, garlic and parsley, then gently toss everything together.

When the *fideua* is ready, the pasta should be cooked and there should be a bit of stocky residue in the pan. Check the seasoning, then remove from the heat and leave to sit for a minute or two before serving. Spoon out the *fideua* and top with some fish.

GNOCCHI AND SQUASH WITH WALNUT AND SAGE SAUCE

This is a fantastically autumnal dish; there is something super-comforting about the texture of gnocchi. Although I do on occasion make my own, usually with spinach or pumpkin, I am very happy with commercially made gnocchi. We are very fortunate to have such a wide range of squash and pumpkin to choose from now. Search out your favourite varieties: some can be quite dry and good for roasting, while others can be watery and are better for a soup, mash or purée. Either type work pretty well here, although I prefer a drier one to contrast with the giving texture of the gnocchi. Squash keeps well, so don't worry that a larger squash will go to waste if you are cooking just for yourself – simply remove the seeds, but leave the skin on, and it should last in the fridge for several days.

For 1

175g (6oz) squash, such as
Crown Prince or Cream of
the Crop
100g (3½oz) gnocchi
30g (⅓ cup) walnuts
1 large clove garlic, crushed
4 sage leaves, shredded

1 tbsp cider vinegar
about 4 tbsp light olive oil
15g (1 tbsp) butter
sea salt and black pepper
10g (3 tbsp) freshly grated
parmesan, to serve
(optional)

Peel and deseed the squash and cut it into gnocchi-sized pieces. Bring a large pan of salted water to the boil and cook the squash until almost tender, then add the gnocchi and cook for the time instructed on the packet, usually 2–3 minutes.

Meanwhile, lightly toast the walnuts in a dry frying pan over a medium heat, watching them very carefully as a scorched walnut is bitter and not much fun to eat. When they are cool enough to handle, rub off their skins, then put into the goblet of a stick blender – this is probably the easiest way with such a small amount, but an upright blender or small food processor should work too. Add the garlic, sage and vinegar and blend to a rough paste, then slowly pour in 3 tablespoons olive oil and keep blending until you have an emulsified sauce. Season with salt and pepper.

When the gnocchi and squash are cooked, drain them well. Heat the butter and a splash of olive oil in a frying pan, then add the gnocchi and squash and brown them for a minute or two. Add the walnut sauce and stir to amalgamate everything. Spoon into a warm bowl and serve with a scattering of parmesan, if you like.

ORECCHIETTE, ROAST RADICCHIO, PEAR AND GORGONZOLA

Radicchio gets a bit of a raw deal, I think. It tends to get put into salad mixes because it's hardy and won't spoil as quickly as some other leaves. Although this wonderfully bitter leaf does work fabulously in salads, especially with cheese or a rich dressing as its foil, I particularly like it roasted. It works brilliantly as an accompaniment to grilled fish and meat, or thrown in with a pot-roast chicken – one of my regular weeknight dishes is a roast radicchio and red wine risotto. For this warming bowl of pasta, a rich velvety sauce is given punch and crunch with some roast radicchio, pear and rosemary. Viva the purple leaf!

For 3

1 small head of radicchio	white wine
2 pears	120ml (½ cup) vegetable or
small sprig of rosemary	chicken stock
2 tbsp light olive oil	100g (3½oz) gorgonzola
1 shallot, finely sliced	180ml (¾ cup) crème fraîche
2 tbsp sherry vinegar	270g (9½oz) orecchiette
100ml (generous ⅓ cup)	sea salt and black pepper

Preheat the oven to 200°C/400°F/gas 6.

Trim the radicchio, cut in half through the core and cut each half into six wedges. Peel, core and quarter the pears. Strip the leaves from the rosemary sprig and chop them. Spread all three across a large baking tray and drizzle over the olive oil. Season well with salt and pepper and give the whole lot a good mix around, then roast in the oven for 10 minutes or until the radicchio is soft and floppy and the pears have a little colour.

Meanwhile, put the shallot in a pan with the sherry vinegar over a medium heat and let it bubble until the vinegar has completely evaporated. Add the wine and reduce by two thirds, then add the stock and simmer until reduced by half. Crumble in the gorgonzola and stir until it has melted. Add the crème fraîche and season with pepper. Simmer for 5 minutes, then use a stick blender (or upright blender) to blend to a smooth sauce.

Bring a large pan of salted water to the boil and cook the orecchiette as instructed on the packet. Drain the pasta and return it to the pan, then pour in the sauce. Stir over a very low heat, just to combine, then check the seasoning and finally add the roast radicchio and pear. Serve in warm bowls.

AN ONION SAUCE FOR SPAGHETTI OR LINGUINE

The idea for this seductively simple recipe comes from a very fine individual called Joe Roberts. Our friendship is mainly web-based, where he fills the pages of social media with vibrant talk of India, literature of all sorts, art, his family and, of course, cooking. Of his original recipe, he says: 'I'm interested in very simple cookery right now, but using the best possible ingredients. The black peppercorns are really necessary, and I find that heating them in a dry pan and then grinding them adds a wonderful aroma… This is one of those dishes, like *cacio e pepe*, that is magically more than the sum of its parts.'

For 4

generous splash of extra virgin
    olive oil
6 anchovy fillets
3 large brown onions,
    very finely sliced
3 cloves garlic, finely chopped
about 20 black peppercorns
1 tbsp thyme leaves
1 tsp brown sugar
    (optional)

good splash of cider vinegar
    or sherry vinegar
500g (1lb 2oz) spaghetti
    or linguine
sea salt
70g (1 cup) freshly grated
    pecorino cheese, to serve
    (optional)

Put the olive oil in a heavy-based saucepan with a lid and place over a medium heat. When the oil is hot, add the anchovies and dissolve in the oil by breaking them up with a wooden spoon. Add the onions and garlic, put the lid on the pan, and keep cooking for at least 15 minutes or until the onions are good and brown.

Meanwhile, toast the peppercorns in a dry frying pan until they are aromatic and then grind them quite finely in a pestle and mortar. Add to the pan of onions, along with the thyme leaves. Taste the onions – they should have a sweetness to them. If they don't taste sweet at all, you could add a teaspoonful of brown sugar, but this isn't usually needed. Add the vinegar and check the seasoning, bearing in mind the saltiness of the anchovies. Add the pecorino, if you're going to be using it (Joe says he finds this just as good without the cheese). The sauce should have a delicious '*agrodolce*', or sour-sweet, taste.

Cook the pasta as instructed on the packet (Joe usually goes for a minute less than the suggested cooking time). Drain well, then stir through the onion sauce and serve – with grated pecorino on the side, if you like.

Excellent eggs

*A time-honoured shortcut to simple dishes for the soul —
and the clear choice for the lone diner.*

Eggs are a Sunday-night no-brainer. Even if I'm not tempted by one of the easy recipes in this chapter, a couple of eggs always make my heart sing. Sunday-night supper was always my dad's domain and, like so many dads, he was a fantastic egg maestro. One of his all-time favourites was an egg cooked in the same coddler he had eaten from as a kid in little round specs and shorts.

SPINACH AND GOAT'S CHEESE SOUFFLÉ OMELETTE

A soufflé omelette takes a bit longer to make than your average omelette, but is well worth the extra effort for its luxurious, cloud-like texture. This makes a perfect solo meal – and perhaps the upgrade to the omelette even warrants a glass of something fizzy instead of Elizabeth David's classic combination of an omelette and a glass of wine… Yes, I think so.

For 1

80g (1½ cups) baby spinach leaves
2 eggs, separated
splash of grapeseed or sunflower oil
small clutch of chives

50g (1¾oz) soft, mild goat's cheese
20g (1½ tbsp) butter
1 tbsp freshly grated parmesan
sea salt and black pepper

Preheat the grill (broiler) to its highest setting.

Wash the spinach, then place in a pan with a splash of oil and cook over a low to medium heat until just wilted – the water clinging to the leaves should be enough to stop it drying out. Drain the spinach in a sieve, pressing with the back of a spoon to squeeze out as much excess water as possible.

Put the spinach in a bowl and, using a fork, mash it a little to break it up. Add the egg yolks, then crumble in the goat's cheese and snip in the chives. Whisk everything together with the fork and season well with salt and pepper. In another bowl, whisk the egg whites to stiff peaks with a pinch of salt, then gently fold into the spinach-yolk mixture.

Heat the butter and a splash of oil in a frying pan with a heatproof handle over a low heat. When it is hot and foaming but not brown, add the egg mixture to the pan. Keep loosening the edges with a palette knife until the omelette is starting to set. Now sprinkle over the parmesan and put the pan under the grill for about 5 minutes to set the top half of the omelette, leaving a slightly *baveuse* ('runny') middle. As soon as your omelette has reached that stage, loosen the edges once again, then fold in half and turn out onto a plate.

BOMBAY POTATOES AND
A FRIED EGG

This simple potato dish packs a nice little punch on a misty autumnal night. A spoonful of yoghurt will mellow it a little, but you may not find that necessary. Breaking the yolk of a fried egg into spuds is always a treat!

For 2

2 potatoes, about 400g (14oz) in total, peeled and cut into 4-cm (1½-in) chunks
2 tbsp sunflower or grapeseed oil
generous pinch of cumin seeds
½ tsp mustard seeds
1 onion, finely sliced
4-cm (1½-in) piece ginger, finely grated
3 garlic cloves, finely grated
½ red chilli, finely chopped
½ tsp ground turmeric
1 tsp ground coriander
¾ tsp ground cumin
½ tsp garam masala
pinch of chilli powder
100ml (generous ⅓ cup) tomato passata
2 eggs
small knob of butter
small handful of coriander (cilantro), roughly chopped
sea salt
2 tbsp Greek-style yoghurt, to serve (optional)

Boil the potatoes in well-salted water until just tender, about 8 minutes.

Meanwhile, heat the oil in a large frying pan over a low to medium heat. Add the cumin and mustard seeds and, when the cumin seeds start to darken slightly, add the onion. Once the onion begins to turn golden brown, add the ginger, garlic, fresh chilli and all the ground spices. Fry gently for a couple of minutes until aromatic, then add the tomato passata. Stir well, then bring to a simmer and cook for 5 minutes.

Drain the potatoes, shaking them about a bit in the colander to rough up their edges, then tip into the frying pan and cook for 3–5 minutes so they absorb the flavours, adding a little warm water if they start to stick. Leave the potatoes ticking away while you fry the eggs in a separate frying pan in a little bit of butter.

When ready to serve, stir most of the chopped coriander into the potatoes and check the seasoning. Divide the potatoes between two warm plates, slide a fried egg onto each one, then scatter over the remaining coriander. Serve with yoghurt on the side, if you like.

EGGS IN A PESTLE AND MORTAR

This recipe comes from my very dear friend Antonio. I have known him since I lived in Granada many years ago, when we both belonged to a group of friends who were really into food – they showed me all the best tapas places. A wonderful cook and bon viveur, he made this for me from his family recipe and I loved it. Ñora peppers are traditionally used to make chorizo, but if you can't find them, just use any other dried pepper or a couple of dried chillies. Spaniards eat these eggs with bread and salad – green or tomato, depending on the time of year.

For 3

80ml (⅓ cup) extra virgin
    olive oil
3 large cloves garlic, peeled
    but left whole
1 dried pepper, ideally a ñora
    pepper, or 1–2 dried chillies

4 eggs
20ml (4 tsp) sherry vinegar
sea salt
toast or bread and salad,
    to serve

Heat the oil in a frying pan over a medium heat and add 2 cloves of garlic and the dried pepper. Be careful when frying these – if the pepper or garlic burns, they become unpalatable and will ruin the whole dish, so keep moving them about in the pan until the pepper has softened and turned slightly darker, but not black, and the garlic is golden. Quickly take the pan off the heat and use a slotted spoon to transfer the garlic and pepper to a large pestle and mortar (or a food processor), leaving the infused oil in the pan. Add the remaining raw clove of garlic to the mortar or food processor and crush or blitz everything to a paste.

Return the frying pan with the oil to the heat and fry the eggs until the whites are properly set, then add them to the pestle and mortar, along with the sherry vinegar and half of the infused oil from the frying pan. Mash everything together: the egg yolks will sort of emulsify everything and you'll end up with a thin paste. (You could do this in the food processor too, but only on pulse.) Check for seasoning and add more of the infused oil or vinegar if you think it needs it.

Serve with toast or bread and a green salad, and prepare to be amazed that something so seemingly unconventional can taste so utterly delicious.

BAKED MUSHROOMS AND EGGS

This dish makes a wonderful Sunday-night supper – or lunch or breakfast. I vary the kind of mushrooms I use according to the season and what I can find: in the autumn, weather permitting, a mixture of chestnut mushrooms and penny buns (*cèpes* in French, *porcini* in Italian) would be my absolute favourite. I have called for a proportionately greater weight of wild mushrooms here, since they tend to need more trimming and cleaning. Save any trimmings if you can, wash them thoroughly and use to make a delicious stock – or leave in a very low oven until completely dried and then whizz to a powder to add to soups, stews or gravies. Depending on which wild mushrooms I use, I might also substitute parsley for the tarragon.

For 4
1 tbsp light olive oil
50g (3½ tbsp) butter
2 shallots, finely sliced
6 flat mushrooms, or 450g
    (1lb) chestnut or button
    mushrooms, or 570g
    (1¼ lb) wild mushrooms,
    cleaned, trimmed and cut
    into bite-sized pieces

3 sprigs tarragon, leaves
    picked and chopped
4 tbsp crème fraîche
4 eggs
sea salt and black pepper
toast and salad, to serve

Preheat the oven to 180°C/350°F/gas 4 and butter four small ramekins about 8cm (3¼ in) in diameter.

Heat the oil and a generous knob of butter in a large frying pan over a low heat. Add the shallots with a pinch of salt and cook gently for about 7 minutes to soften, stirring regularly to stop them burning. Add all the remaining butter except for a tiny nut to the pan, along with the mushrooms. Turn up the heat to medium and fry the mushrooms until they get a bit of colour. Keep cooking, moving them around so they cook evenly, until they start to soften and release their liquid – let this evaporate. Remove from the heat, then add the tarragon and season with salt and pepper.

Divide the mushrooms between the ramekins, then spoon in half the crème fraîche. Make a dip in each ramekin and crack in an egg, being careful not to break the yolk. Season with salt and pepper, then spoon over the rest of the crème fraîche.

Bake in the oven for about 15 minutes, or until the egg whites are properly cooked but the yolks are still runny. Serve straight away, with toast and salad on the side.

SCRAMBLED EGGS
WITH BLACK PUDDING

I am a big fan of morcilla. This Spanish blood sausage has a slightly softer texture than its English counterpart of black pudding, and a really good hum of nutmeg. If you can get hold of some, I would highly recommend it for this cheeky little supper, which has become a regular Sunday-nighter for me. As such, I have developed a canny one-pan method of cooking it, so the black pudding doesn't turn the eggs a weird grey-ish colour.

For 2
100g (3½oz) black pudding
  or morcilla
splash of sunflower
  or grapeseed oil
4 eggs

3 tbsp water
20g (1½ tbsp) butter
sea salt and black pepper
2 thick slices toast of your
  choice, to serve

Remove the outer casing from the black pudding or morcilla, then crumble it.

Heat the oil in a large heavy-based frying pan. Add the black pudding, keeping it to one side of the pan.

Crack the eggs into a bowl, add the water and beat lightly, then season with salt and pepper.

Throw the butter into the other side of the pan, then carefully pour the eggs onto the butter side of the pan and stir gently to scramble, keeping them on their side of the pan. By now, over on its side of the pan, the black pudding should be well warmed through. When the eggs are very nearly cooked, mix both sides together, taking care not to do it too much so you retain some nice nuggets of black pudding.

Pile onto hot buttered toast and serve straight away.

CODDLED EGG IVANHOE

We ate a lot of coddled eggs on Sunday nights in my childhood, I think maybe because they're such an easy thing to do and yet so deeply comforting to eat. Egg coddlers have a delightful air of nostalgia about them: one I remember fondly was a small china pot with a metal lid that had been my father's since his childhood, so the sentimentality appealed to me, plus it was very pretty! These days they can still be hunted down, but if you have no luck a ramekin or small jam jar makes a good stand-in, especially if it has a lid (or a covering of foil will also work). The coddled egg is aided and abetted by a steamy environment, resulting in a texture similar to that of a poached egg, with a set white and runny yolk, in contrast to the firmer texture of baked eggs (see page 61).

'Ivanhoe' is a garnish I came across in Robin McDouall's wonderful *Clubland Cooking*. It involves cream and smoked haddock, which I cook as instructed by Polly Russell, my dearest friend and co-conspirator on *The Kitchen Revolution*. Any other smoked fish would work here: my favourite is super-decadent smoked eel, which needs a touch less butter, and probably horseradish in place of the mustard.

For 1

75g (2¾oz) smoked haddock or other smoked fish
20ml (1½ tbsp) double (heavy) cream
1 tsp dijon mustard
small handful of flat-leaf parsley, finely chopped

20g (1½ tbsp) butter, melted
1 large egg – a duck egg would be splendid
sea salt and black pepper
1 thick slice toast of your choice, to serve

Start by cooking the smoked haddock. (If using another smoked fish, it may not need cooking – in which case, you can just flake the flesh and skip ahead to the next step.) Put the fish in a shallow heatproof dish with a lid, season with a little salt and a generous grinding of pepper and cover with freshly boiled water. Put the lid on the dish and leave to stand: by the time the fish is cool enough to handle, it will be cooked. Flake the fish, removing any skin and bones. (The fish-cooking liquor has excellent flavour and is worth keeping for anything you might need fish stock for – just bring it to the boil before chilling and then freezing in ice-cube trays, ready to be dropped into fish soups, etc.)

continued overleaf

Meanwhile, mix the cream, mustard and parsley together. Grease the egg coddler, jar or ramekin well with melted butter, then stir the rest of the butter into the parsley and cream mixture, together with the flaked smoked fish. Put two thirds of the fish mixture in the coddler, crack an egg on top and lightly scatter the rest of the fish mixture on top, being careful not to to break the yolk. Put the lid on the coddler or cover the ramekin tightly with foil; if using a jam jar, screw the lid on, but don't tighten it too much.

Half-fill a saucepan with water and bring to a gentle simmer, then carefully lower the coddler into the pan – the water should come about two-thirds of the way up the sides of the coddler. Cook for 5–6 minutes or until the egg white has just set. Serve immediately with hot buttered toast.

TOASTED SPAGHETTI WITH RED ONIONS, ALMONDS AND RAISINS

(see page 47)

RICHARD'S CRAB LINGUINE

(see page 50)

CATALAN ANGEL-HAIR PASTA WITH SEAFOOD

(see page 51)

EGGS IN A PESTLE AND MORTAR

(see page 60)

CODDLED EGG IVANHOE

(see page 63)

MEXICAN OMELETTE

(see page 68)

SATSUMA, POMEGRANATE, FENNEL AND
CHICORY SALAD WITH FETA

(see page 74)

QUICK SOUSED MACKEREL WITH
BREAD-AND-BUTTER PICKLES

(see page 76)

BACON AND EGG PIE

Bacon and egg pie is an absolute New Zealand staple and, as my mum is a Kiwi, this pie featured heavily in my youth, made in the same enamel pie plate I now have and use. It always came on picnics with us, wrapped in newspaper straight from the oven to keep it hot until lunchtime, so my memories are of a warm, slightly soggy pie with a hint of newsprint! Which mightn't sound great, but trust me, it really, really was. At my first solo cooking venture, the Sutton Arms pub in Smithfield, I put the pie on as a bar snack. It was cooked in a little black steel frying pan as an individual portion, and was so popular we could hardly keep up with the pastry making. I tend to eat this simply with chutney or ketchup, but buttered peas or a salad would also work, and would help make the pie stretch to four servings.

For 3–4
200g (7oz) all-butter puff
   pastry
small nut of butter
5 eggs

4 rashers of back bacon,
   rind removed
sea salt and black pepper

Preheat the oven to 210°C/425°F/gas 6–7, putting a baking sheet in to heat at the same time. Grease a 22cm (9in) pie plate or cake tin.

Roll out the pastry to a thickness of about 3mm (⅛in) and cut out two circles about 24cm (9½in) in diameter, one for the bottom and one for the top. Line the pie plate with pastry, pressing it well into the base and draping any excess over the sides. Crack the eggs into the pie – sometimes, depending on the size of the eggs, I hold back a bit of the white of the last egg in case it threatens to overflow. Use the tip of a small-bladed knife to pierce each yolk, then give the eggs a good dousing of salt and pepper. Lay the bacon on top. Paint the rim of the pie, either using the bit of egg white you held back or by just dipping your pastry brush in the filling; also paint the top of the other circle of pastry and cut a cross in its centre. Carefully lay the other circle of pastry on top of the pie, painted side up, and press the edges together very well. Trim off the excess overhanging pastry, then go round the rim of the pie pressing with the tines of a fork, or crimp between finger and thumb if you're feeling super-fancy.

Put the pie on the hot baking sheet and turn the oven down to 190°C/375°F/gas 5. Cook the pie for about 25 minutes, by which time the eggs should be set and the bacon cooked. Take the pie out of the oven and carefully slide it out of its plate and onto a wire rack, so the crisp bottom you have engineered doesn't start steaming in the dish and go soggy. Serve hot or warm.

SOFT-BOILED EGG WITH ASPARAGUS SOLDIERS

In a Cambridgeshire village near the one where I live, there's the most wondrous asparagus grower called Peter Elliot. He has been doing it forever, man and boy, and he regularly threatens to retire. When he does, I will be quite bereft, as his is the best asparagus I have ever come across. I particularly love his ramshackle 'processing plant', a corrugated-iron barn full of remarkable Heath Robinson-esque contraptions for putting elastic bands on bunches and suchlike. I flatly refuse to eat asparagus outside its season – traditionally from St George's Day, 23 April, to the end of May (I'm telling you this because some growers seem to be popping it out in February these days, and I find it all most sinister) – but for those few precious weeks it appears at every meal possible. At other times of year, this addictive parmesan crusting can be used for salsify and celeriac in winter, or purple sprouting broccoli in early spring (bit more unwieldy to dip into an egg, mind you).

For 4
400g (14oz) asparagus
30g (2 tbsp) butter
30g (½ cup) panko or
  other breadcrumbs
finely grated zest ¼ lemon
  (optional)

pinch of cayenne pepper
60g (1 cup) freshly grated
  parmesan
1 large egg white
4 eggs
sea salt

Preheat the oven to 200°C/400°F/gas 6.

Bring a pan of salted water to the boil. Snap the woody ends off the asparagus, then blanch the spears in the boiling water for about a minute and drain well. The asparagus will, of course, finish cooking in the oven later, but I prefer to take the raw edge off it first. If you're short of time, though, you could skip this step.

Meanwhile, melt the butter and lightly brush a baking tray with a little of it. Pour the rest of the butter into a wide, shallow dish and add the breadcrumbs, lemon zest (if using), cayenne, a pinch of salt and all except 2 tablespoons of the parmesan. Mix well. In another bowl, lightly whisk the egg white with a pinch of salt, just to break it down enough to coat the asparagus spears.

Toss the asparagus spears first in the egg white and then in the parmesan crumbs, coating them well. Place them on the buttered baking tray in a single layer.

Put the tray in the oven and bake the asparagus until just beginning to brown, about 5 minutes. Turn the tray around if some spears seem more golden than others, then scatter over the remaining 2 tablespoons of parmesan and cook for another 6–8 minutes or until golden and crisp.

When the asparagus is coming up to its last few minutes in the oven, bring a saucepan of water to the boil and soft-boil the eggs.

Serve the eggs in egg cups, with the asparagus soldiers alongside, ready for dipping in the yolk.

MEXICAN OMELETTE

I first had this while staying with my dear friend Chloe and her son in Austin, Texas, where the Mexican food is a very different beast from the watered-down versions we tend to get in the UK – super-tasty and pretty naughty. This omelette isn't a bad boy, but still has those gutsy flavours going on. I like to make a simple guacamole to go with this: just finely chopped red onion, plenty of lime juice and salt, avocado and chopped coriander roughly mashed together. The style of the omelette itself is more Spanish than French: after an initial stirring, you can leave it to cook, just loosening the edges as it sets.

For 2
2 soft corn tortillas
about 2 tbsp extra virgin
    olive oil
pinch of chilli powder
small handful of coriander
    (cilantro), finely chopped
2 large plum tomatoes,
    roughly chopped

3 spring onions (scallions),
    trimmed and finely sliced
1 large green chilli, finely
    chopped
4 large eggs
50g (½ cup) grated cheddar
sea salt

Stack the tortillas together and cut them into strips to make tortilla 'ribbons'. Heat the oil in a heavy-based saucepan over a medium heat and, when it's hot, drop in the tortilla ribbons. Fry until golden and crisp, then lift out and drain well. Season with salt and a tiny bit of chilli powder and mix with the coriander.

Leave the pan on the heat – there should still be a coating of oil in the pan, but if not add a splash more. Add the tomatoes, spring onions and chopped chilli and fry for a couple of minutes, stirring from time to time. Crack the eggs into a bowl, then beat lightly and season with salt and chilli powder. Pour into the pan and stir to amalgamate everything, then sprinkle over the cheese and turn the heat down to low. When the omelette is nearly set, scatter over the crispy tortilla strips.
Once it's fully set, cut in half and serve on warm plates.

Comfort light

*For warmer Sunday nights – or when you've had a
mega-blow-out weekend.*

Long summer evenings spent outside in the garden, or on a balcony or rooftop,
just letting life wash over you and prolonging the weekend until well after the
light has finally gone – these are the perfect times for the dishes in this chapter.
But on less delightful evenings weather-wise, a lighter meal can be a way of
looking ahead to brighter days, or perhaps remembering a happy holiday. And
sometimes your body needs or yearns for the crisp crunch of a good salad or
vegetable-based dish for a boost to body and soul.

WATERCRESS AND BEETROOT SALAD WITH HORSERADISH DRESSING AND A BOILED EGG

This salad is pretty much an assembly job once you have all the component parts to hand. You can, of course, buy ready-cooked beetroot, though I must admit I prefer to cook a batch myself and keep them in the fridge, where they'll last well for up to a week. If you want to do the same, put your washed beetroots in an ovenproof dish with a splash each of olive oil and cider vinegar, a sprig or two of thyme and a bay leaf, and some salt and pepper. Then pour in enough water to generously cover the base, perhaps with a bit of apple juice thrown in for luck, cover the dish tightly with foil and cook in a 150°C/300°F/gas 2 oven for a good hour or until they feel soft when pierced with a knife. Wait until the beetroots are cool enough to handle before slipping the skins off. This salad is delicious with some smoked fish flaked through it, or with boiled new potatoes instead of the croutons, if you want something more substantial.

For 2
20g (⅓ cup) croutons,
  shop-bought or homemade
  from stale bread
2 eggs
1 large cooked beetroot (beet)
25g (½ cup) baby spinach
  leaves
30g (⅔ cup) watercress, any
  coarse stems removed
sea salt and black pepper

For the horseradish dressing
1 tsp finely grated fresh
  horseradish root or jarred
  horseradish
100ml (generous ⅓ cup)
  crème fraîche
juice of ½ lemon

If you're making your own croutons, cut a thick slice of stale bread into chunky squares, toss in some olive oil and black pepper and bake at 180°C/350°F/gas 4 for 10–15 minutes or until crisp and golden.

To make the horseradish dressing, mix the horseradish with the crème fraîche and lemon juice, then season very well with salt and pepper.

Boil the eggs to your liking – I usually give them 6 minutes for 'fudgey' yolks. Plunge straight into cold running water, then peel and cut in half.

Cut the beetroot into small wedges, then put into a large bowl, together with the croutons, spinach and watercress. Season with salt and pepper, then pour over the dressing and gently toss everything together.

Pile the salad onto two plates and top with the egg halves – I like to season the yolks with salt and pepper.

SATSUMA, POMEGRANATE, FENNEL AND CHICORY SALAD WITH FETA

Pomegranates and satsumas come into season around the same time in late autumn and make very good partners, with their different notes of sharp and sweet. This salad is ideal for the crisp and cold evenings we get at this time of year, especially when eaten with some warm flatbread or pitta bread to mop up all the juices. It would also make a lovely starter before a rich main course.

My greatest friend, Imogen, tells me her mum would keep her and her sisters quiet as children by giving them a quarter of a pomegranate and a pin each and leaving them to pick out the seeds individually and eat them, resulting in hours of concentration for the kids – and hours of peace for their mum!

For 4

6 satsumas	2 fennel bulbs
1 small red onion, very finely sliced	200g (7oz) feta
1 large pomegranate	3 heads of chicory (Belgian endive), leaves separated
1½ tbsp red wine vinegar	small bunch of chives, finely chopped
1 tsp honey	sea salt and black pepper
4 tbsp extra virgin olive oil	

Peel the satsumas with a knife to get rid of all the pith, then cut into slices about 3mm (⅛in) thick. Put the satsuma slices, along with any juices, into a large bowl with the onion and a pinch of salt. Mix well, then leave to soften down while you tackle the pomegranate.

Cut the pomegranate in half, then cut one half in half again. Squeeze the juice from the two quarters through a sieve into a bowl – you may need to do a bit of prodding with a fork to get the pomegranate to release its juice. This should reward you with about 4 tablespoons of pomegranate juice. Add the red wine vinegar and honey to the bowl, then season with salt and pepper. Slowly drizzle in the oil, whisking to incorporate into the dressing.

Take the other half of the pomegranate, place it cut-side down on a board and tap it with a rolling pin to dislodge the seeds. Remove any white membrane from the seeds, then add them to the bowl with the satsumas and onion. Trim the fennel, keeping any fronds, then slice very finely and add to the bowl. Chop the reserved fennel fronds and add these too. Now crumble in the feta and gently toss all the ingredients together.

Put the chicory leaves and chives in another bowl, season lightly and dress with some of the pomegranate dressing. Arrange the chicory leaves on four plates, then scatter the rest of the salad over the top, finishing with some extra dressing.

QUICK SOUSED MACKEREL WITH
BREAD-AND-BUTTER PICKLES

When I say quick I don't mean immediate, but this light summer supper is do-able in a day if you souse the mackerel and make the pickles in the morning to eat that evening. You could also use herrings, sardines or anchovies here. My friend Laura Jackson, co-founder of a wonderful cafe on the Regent's Canal in East London called Towpath, was my inspiration for this dish – she is a great pickler and always has some deliciously vibrant pickles on the menu.

For 2
2 slices of rye bread
60ml (¼ cup) crème fraîche
fronds from 3 stalks of dill,
   finely chopped
sea salt

For the soused mackerel
1 small carrot, cut into
   thin rounds
1 small fennel bulb, trimmed
   and finely sliced
1 banana shallot, finely sliced
1 tsp coriander seeds
1 tsp fennel seeds
½ tsp black peppercorns
4 juniper berries
6 tbsp sugar
300ml (1¼ cups) white wine
   vinegar
4 mackerel fillets, cleaned

For the bread-and-butter
   pickles
1 small head chicory (Belgian
   endive), cut lengthways into
   six wedges
1 small red onion, finely sliced
½ small cucumber, peeled
   and finely sliced
½ kohlrabi, peeled and
   finely sliced
250ml (1 cup) cider vinegar
125g (scant ⅔ cup) sugar
1 bay leaf
juice and zest of ½ lemon,
   peeled off in strips

For the soused mackerel, put the carrot, fennel, shallot, coriander and fennel seeds, peppercorns, juniper berries, sugar and 1 teaspoon of salt in a saucepan. Pour in the vinegar and 300ml (1¼ cups) water and bring to the boil, then simmer gently for 10 minutes, or until the carrot is just cooked.

Pat the mackerel fillets dry and place flesh-side down in a shallow glass or ceramic dish. Pour over the sousing liquid and leave to cool, then cover with cling film and refrigerate for at least 6 hours.

Next make the bread-and-butter pickles. Take a lidded glass jar or plastic container big enough to hold all the vegetables and put in the chicory, followed by the onion, then the cucumber and the kohlrabi. Put the vinegar, sugar, lemon juice and zest into a small stainless steel saucepan. Bring to the boil, then simmer for 3 minutes. Pour the hot pickling liquor over the vegetables, then seal the container and leave to cool before refrigerating. The pickles are ready after 6–8 hours, but will improve with a few days or even a couple of weeks under their belts.

When you want to eat, lift the mackerel fillets from the sousing liquid and cut in half. Toast the rye bread and serve with the fish and pickles, a dollop of crème fraîche and a scattering of dill.

SMOKED CHICKEN, GREEN BEAN AND BORLOTTI BEAN SALAD WITH FIG DRESSING

In early summer, when the local fig trees start to come into leaf, I usually pick some of the tender young leaves and steep them in some cider vinegar or white wine vinegar for a couple of weeks. The infused vinegar imparts the most delicious flavour to salad dressings. I've used dried figs in a similar way here, for a more autumnal salad – but if you happen to have some fig-leaf vinegar, by all means use that, or try it with fresh figs in late summer. I also make an elderflower vinegar, which I use in dressings or marinades for fish and poultry.

For 4
100g (3½oz) green beans,
    topped and tailed
400g (14oz) fresh borlotti
    beans in pods or half a 400g
    (14oz) tin of borlottis
25g (¼ cup) walnuts
1 good-sized butterhead
    lettuce, leaves separated
400g (14oz) smoked chicken
    meat, shredded
sea salt and black pepper
bread, to serve

For the fig dressing
30g (¼ cup) dried figs,
    any hard tops removed
1½ tbsp sherry vinegar
1 generous tbsp dijon mustard
1½ tbsp extra virgin
    olive oil
90ml (⅓ cup) grapeseed or
    sunflower oil

For the fig dressing, soak the dried figs in boiling water for 10 minutes, then drain. Pour the vinegar over the figs and leave to infuse for about 30 minutes. Transfer the figs and vinegar into a small food processor, add the mustard and whizz until smooth. With the motor running, slowly drizzle in both oils to form a nice emulsified dressing. Season with salt and pepper.

Bring a saucepan of salted water to the boil and, when the water is at a rolling boil, throw in the green beans and cook until they are just tender, about 4 minutes. Lift out the beans and plunge them into cold water to refresh, so they keep their bright green colour, then drain well. If using fresh borlotti beans, pod them and then cook for 10 minutes in the boiling water. Remove from the heat and leave to cool in the water, then drain well. If using tinned borlottis, give them a good rinse and drain well.

Toast the walnuts under a hot grill (broiler) or in a 180°C/350°F/gas 4 oven for about 3 minutes, or until the skins come away easily. While they are still warm, wrap in a clean tea towel or some kitchen paper and give them a rub to take off the skins and break them up a little.

Put the lettuce leaves into a large serving bowl with the beans, walnuts, chicken and a little salt and pepper. Add some of the dressing and gently toss everything together, then add more dressing to taste. Serve the salad straight away, with bread for mopping up the juices.

JACK'S LIFE-GIVING SOUP

A dear friend and one of my favourite cooks, Jack has fed me this soup on many occasions, and I'm always blown away by how uplifting it is – hence the name! It's a busy cook's dream soup: complex in flavour, yet simple in preparation. It is all the more wonderful in that most of the ingredients are from the store-cupboard; you just need to pick up whatever you fancy adding.

For 2–3

1 x 400ml (14 fl oz) tin of proper coconut milk – I suggest Aroy-D
1 banana shallot, finely chopped
3 dried red chillies, preferably bird's eye, crumbled
3 fresh or frozen kaffir lime leaves (optional)
2 tbsp fish sauce
100g (6½ tbsp) tamarind paste
75g (4 tbsp) fermented black bean paste
1½ tbsp sugar, ideally palm sugar

protein suggestions: pork mince, thinly sliced raw pork fillet (tenderloin), sliced raw chicken breast, prawns, cubed tofu, soft-boiled egg
vegetable suggestions: mange-tout (snow peas), aubergine (eggplant), mushrooms, deseeded cucumber, asparagus, courgette (zucchini)
100g (3½oz) dried fine rice noodles
sea salt
small handful of coriander (cilantro) or Thai basil, to serve (optional)

Pour the coconut milk into a large saucepan, then fill the can with water to rinse it out and add this to the pan, along with the shallot and chillies. If you are adding kaffir lime leaves, and I suggest you do, now would be the time. Bring to a gentle simmer and cook for a few minutes, then add the fish sauce, tamarind paste and fermented black bean paste – feel free to add more than the suggested amounts. Balance out the tartness of the tamarind with a little sugar – ideally palm sugar, but as the other flavours are so punchy, brown or even regular white sugar substitute well. Add your chosen protein and vegetables and heat until cooked through. Check the seasoning.

Soak the noodles in freshly boiled water with a pinch of salt for a few minutes, just to rehydrate them. When they are supple, drain well and divide between two or three bowls, then pour in the hot soup and serve. Chopped coriander or Thai basil would be welcome finishing touches, but are by no means essential.

SMOKED CHICKEN, GREEN BEAN AND
BORLOTTI BEAN SALAD WITH FIG DRESSING

(see page 78)

JACK'S LIFE-GIVING SOUP

(see page 80)

CHICKEN HARIRA

(see page 86)

PORK AND CASHEW NUT STIR-FRY

(see page 90)

PIZZA BY ANY OTHER NAME

(see page 94)

TERRAZZO & ANCHOVY STUFFED EGGS

(see pages 110 & 111)

TRAINWRECK & WHITE BEAN CROQUETTES
WITH HERBY MAYONNAISE

(see pages 114 & 115)

LIGHT EMITTING DIODE & SQUASH
& TRUFFLE BRANDADE

(see pages 103 & 104)

A COMFORTING BOWL OF DHAL

This comes from my wonderful friend and clever cook Lucas Hollweg – I love the way he writes recipes, and this is no exception: simple, thoughtful and delicious. As Lucas says, the puy lentils aren't even remotely traditional here, but they do bring variety to the texture: the comforting mush of the red, the residual bite of the green.

For 4

150g (scant 1 cup) red
*   split lentils*
150g (¾ cup) puy lentils
4 tbsp vegetable oil
3 medium onions, finely sliced
5 cloves garlic, peeled but
*   left whole*
4-cm (1½-in) piece of ginger,
*   peeled and roughly chopped*
6 cardamom pods, bashed
1 tbsp ground cumin
1 tbsp garam masala

1 tsp ground turmeric
1 tsp ground coriander
¼ tsp chilli powder
1 tsp sugar
3 handfuls of coriander
*   (cilantro), roughly chopped*
couple of squeezes of
*   lemon juice*
sea salt
rice, to serve (optional)
4 generous tbsp yoghurt,
*   to serve*

Put both kinds of lentils in a saucepan with 1.25 litres (5 cups) of water – don't add any salt. Bring to the boil, then simmer for 25–30 minutes, or until the lentils are tender.

Heat 3 tablespoons of the oil in a frying pan and cook the onions over a medium heat for 15 minutes, stirring often, until they are brown and partly caramelized. Tip into a bowl and set aside.

Put the garlic and ginger in a blender with 3 tablespoons of water and whizz to a paste.

Heat the remaining tablespoon of oil in the frying pan over a medium heat, add the cardamom pods and stir for 1 minute. Add the garlic and ginger paste and cook for 2–3 minutes, or until the liquid has evaporated. Add the ground spices and stir for a minute or so, then add the sugar, 2 teaspoons of salt and 100ml (generous ⅓ cup) of water, and keep stirring and cooking until the liquid has evaporated and you have a thick paste.

continued overleaf

Stir in the cooked lentils and onions and let everything bubble away gently for another 10 minutes, adding a splash more water if necessary, until the dhal is thick. Stir in two-thirds of the coriander and a squeeze or two of lemon juice. Taste and add more salt if necessary.

Serve in bowls – on rice, if you want it – with a good dollop of yoghurt and a scattering of coriander on top.

SAM'S SALAD: ROAST CARROT AND SQUASH WITH ORANGE, PUMPKIN SEEDS AND GOAT'S CHEESE

Sam is a great friend who is always highly appreciative of whatever I cook for her. She loves a risotto, but her second favourite is a goat's cheese salad – and she made me promise that if such a thing made an appearance in my book I would name it after her! Her favourite version is with beetroot, which you could easily use instead of the squash, but I was aiming for a wintry salad here, full of rich tastes and warm colours. I absolutely love rainbow carrots – they give such vibrancy to any dish, I think, but you could of course substitute regular carrots.

For 2

40g (¼ cup) pumpkin seeds
400g (14oz) squash –
    butternut is easiest to find,
    but I also like gem, onion or
    Crown Prince
150g (5½oz) rainbow carrots
3 tbsp olive oil
3 sprigs of thyme

1 large orange
2 tsp white balsamic vinegar
2 large handfuls mixed
    salad leaves
60g (2oz) soft fresh goat's
    cheese
sea salt and black pepper

Preheat the oven to 200°C/400°F/gas 6. Toast the pumpkin seeds on a small baking tray in the oven for about 4–5 minutes while it's heating – keep an eye on them as they burn easily. Toss them in a little salt while they are still hot.

Use a large sharp knife to cut the squash in half, then scoop out the seeds and cut into more manageable pieces to peel – a small sturdy knife is generally best for this, as squashes tend to have very tough skins. Once peeled, cut the flesh into 2-cm (¾-in) chunks and put in a large bowl. Peel the carrots and cut into 2-cm (¾-in) chunks, then add to the bowl. Pour the olive oil into the bowl, add the thyme and toss everything together. Peel the orange and segment it over the bowl, catching any juices, and then squeeze any remaining core into the bowl too. Season the vegetables well with salt and pepper. Tip the lot out onto a large non-stick baking tray and spread out evenly. Roast for 20 minutes, or until the squash and carrots are tender and starting to brown. Remove from the oven and leave to cool slightly.

When you are ready to serve, tip the vegetables into a large bowl and lift out the thyme. Add the vinegar and salad leaves, and mix briefly. Crumble in the goat's cheese, then divide between two plates and scatter with the pumpkin seeds.

Remains of the day

I have always been a great patron of the leftover.

Nothing gives me greater pleasure than to use up some of the bits and bobs lurking in the fridge. My very greatest friend's family had a dish they called 'rubbish soup', a brilliant and delicious noodle soup with many fridge orphans dropped in or sprinkled on top. When we were growing up, I loved a Sunday night there, as the family gathered around steaming bowls of flavoursome broth with a variety of little bowls of treats to add in at will – my theory was that you could tell a lot about a person from what they chose!

CHICKEN HARIRA

I love this hearty Middle Eastern-inspired soup. It comes from my days working with Juliet Peston, an amazing chef who ran the kitchen at Alastair Little's in Soho for a long time and was a force to be reckoned with. We worked together for many years, including at Lola's in Islington, where this harira would appear regularly. You can also make it with lamb, so once you have mastered the art of the stew-y bit, it can become a good home for leftover chicken or lamb, or even some roasted veg, from your Sunday roast. The ginger and coriander relish keeps very well and can be added to curries, chillies or other spicy numbers – you might want to make double the amount and keep a jar handy in the fridge. For this recipe you won't need the whole tin of chickpeas, but I figure you could easily knock up a little bit of hummus while the harira is bubbling away (or they could be transmogrified into another meal later in the week).

For 4

about 4 tbsp sunflower
    or grapeseed oil
1 large red onion, sliced
1 red (bell) pepper, deseeded
    and sliced
1 tsp caraway seeds
2 tsp ground cumin
2 heaped tsp ground coriander
2 tsp hot smoked paprika
2 large cloves garlic, crushed
400g (14oz) leftover, shredded
    cooked chicken or 570g
    (1¼ lb) boneless skinless
    chicken thighs, cut into
    bite-sized pieces
2 heaped tsp garam masala
2 tbsp red wine vinegar
1 x 400g (14oz) tin of chopped
    tomatoes
400ml (1⅔ cups) chicken
    or vegetable stock

100g (½ cup) green or
    brown lentils
110g (scant ⅔ cup)
    long-grain rice
160g (1¼ cups) tinned
    chickpeas (garbanzo beans),
    drained but liquid reserved
sea salt
flatbreads, to serve

For the ginger and
coriander relish
8-cm (3-in) piece of ginger,
    peeled and roughly chopped
2 large handfuls of coriander
    (cilantro) leaves
finely grated zest and juice
    of 2 lemons
4 tbsp light olive oil
¼ tsp sea salt

Heat about 2 tablespoons of the oil in a large saucepan over a low heat. Add the onion and a pinch of salt, cover with a lid and sweat until the onion is soft, stirring from time to time to avoid it sticking or getting too brown – a little colour is fine. Add the pepper to the pan, and a touch more oil if needed, and cook for a couple of minutes until beginning to soften. Now add all the spices, except the garam masala, and cook for a minute until aromatic, then add the garlic and stir everything about for a minute – if everything seems a bit dry, a splash more oil wouldn't go amiss.

Meanwhile, toss the chicken in the garam masala. If using raw chicken, season it well with salt as well, then heat a tablespoon of oil in a frying pan and brown it all over before adding it to the saucepan. Deglaze the frying pan by splashing in the red wine vinegar and 200ml (generous ¾ cup) water and stirring and scraping the base of the pan to loosen any meaty bits, then tip into the saucepan. If using leftover cooked chicken, this needs to go in later, so just pour the red wine vinegar and 200 ml (generous ¾ cup) water into the saucepan.

Now add the tomatoes and stock to the saucepan and cook for about 10 minutes. Rinse the lentils and rice in a sieve under cold running water, then add to the pan with another 200ml (generous ¾ cup) water. Cook for 25–30 minutes or until the rice and lentils are cooked, by which time the chicken will be nice and tender too. Throw in the chickpeas and their liquid – and if you are using leftover chicken, add that now too. Leave to simmer for 5 more minutes or until thoroughly heated through.

Whilst the harira is simmering away, whizz all the relish ingredients to a paste in a food processor.

To serve, ladle the harira into bowls and stir in a heaped tablespoon of the relish. Check for seasoning and add more relish if you wish – I often serve this with a little extra dollop on top for people to stir in as they eat. Warm flatbreads are great for scooping up this delicious supper.

PATATAS BRAVAS WITH A FRIED EGG

Finding a few cooked potatoes in the fridge is such a joy because then you can fry them! So I figure a good Sunday night would involve fried leftover potatoes in my favourite Spanish-style tomato sauce with a little kick. 'Top-drawer nosebag!' as my dear friend and stalwart of the London restaurant scene Thomas Blythe would say.

Tinned cherry tomatoes are such a handy store-cupboard staple: they are super-sweet and help to make this tomato sauce a versatile condiment that goes with multiple things, a bit like a lo-fi ketchup. Even better, it will keep well in the fridge for a couple of weeks and you can add fresh herbs, if you like, or spice it up by adding some curry paste or grated ginger at the same time as the garlic.

For 1 – with extra sauce
  for another day
100g (3½oz) cooked potatoes
1½ tbsp extra virgin olive oil
1 egg
sea salt

For the tomato sauce
2 tbsp extra virgin olive oil
2 banana shallots, finely sliced
2 cloves garlic, crushed
generous pinch of chilli powder
1 bay leaf
1 sprig of oregano or about
  1 tsp dried oregano
2 tsp honey
2 tsp sherry vinegar
1 x 400g (14oz) tin of
  cherry tomatoes
3½ tbsp orange juice

To make the tomato sauce, heat the oil in a saucepan over a low heat. Add the shallots, along with a pinch of salt, and cook for about 7 minutes, stirring occasionally, until softened. Add the garlic, chilli, bay leaf and oregano and let the flavours get to know each other for a couple of minutes, stirring often so the onion doesn't catch and brown. Add the honey, sherry vinegar and tomatoes, then rinse out the empty tomato tin with the orange juice and add that to the pan, too. Bring to the boil, then turn down to a simmer and leave to bubble for about 15 minutes or until the sauce has become quite thick and the flavour has intensified, stirring from time to time to prevent sticking. Fish out the bay leaf and oregano sprig, then season with salt to taste.

When the tomato sauce is nearing readiness, cut the potatoes into 2-cm (¾-in) chunks – as rough as you like, then all the edges will get nice and crispy when fried. Heat the oil in a large frying pan over a medium heat until hot, then throw in the spuds and leave for a good few minutes to brown on the first side – it's tempting to get in there and shake them all about, but crispiness comes to those who wait! Once the potatoes are looking nicely brown on the first side, shake them about, and from now on move them more regularly, keeping an eye on the heat, until they are nicely browned and crisp all over, then toss in some salt.

Meanwhile, in another frying pan, fry an egg to your liking.

To serve, pile the spuds onto a plate, top with the egg, sprinkling a pinch of salt on the yolk, then spoon over your rich tomato sauce.

PORK AND CASHEW NUT STIR-FRY

Stir-fries always remind me of student days, when they seemed to be what everyone made – and were often just an excuse to dump the contents of the fridge into a pan. As I was already cooking professionally to earn extra cash, I was never that into them at the time, but have since discovered what a quick and easy supper they make, without becoming a dumping ground for anything and everything! This one is simplicity itself and seems to appeal to adults and kids alike, either served with plain noodles or rice, or just on its own. Once you've mastered this stir-fry, you can use the same flavourings to make endless variations: try chicken and basil, beef and ginger, or fish and garlic.

For 2

2 tbsp sunflower or grapeseed oil
30g (¼ cup) cashew nuts
1 tbsp chilli flakes
4 spring onions (scallions)
200g (7oz) leftover cooked pork or 280g (10oz) pork loin

1 tsp cornflour (cornstarch)
120ml (½ cup) chicken stock
2 tsp red curry paste
2 tbsp fish sauce
2 tbsp lime juice
1 tsp dark brown sugar
2 tsp soy sauce

Heat the oil in a wok or large frying pan and fry the cashews until golden brown, stirring constantly. Lift out with a slotted spoon and drain on kitchen paper, then chop roughly.

Throw the chilli flakes into the frying pan and let them brown. Strain the oil through a fine sieve to catch the chilli flakes and discard them, unless you like seriously spicy food – in which case, mix some or all of them with the cashews.

Slice the spring onions into nice long strands and thinly slice the pork, be it raw or cooked. In a small bowl, mix the cornflour to a smooth paste with a couple of tablespoons of the stock.

Wipe out the wok or pan, pour in the chilli-infused oil and place over a medium to high heat. If using raw pork, add it first, stir-frying it until it changes colour, then add the spring onions. If using leftover cooked pork, just throw it and the spring onions in together and brown very quickly, keeping them moving constantly. Return the cashew nuts to the pan. Next add the curry paste, fish sauce, lime juice, sugar and the rest of the stock and simmer for 10 minutes.

Ladle out a couple of spoonfuls of the sauce and stir into the cornflour paste to loosen it and make it easier to add back to the stir-fry. Pour the paste into the pan and stir for a couple of minutes until the sauce has thickened. Add soy sauce to taste and serve straight away.

BOUILLABAISSE OF
PEAS AND BEANS

This is like an inland version of bouillabaisse, the classic southern French fish soup that I originally came across in Elizabeth David's *French Provincial Cooking* – I love her books and often spend time poring over them. A deliciously simple broth enhanced with saffron and a poached egg, this offers a good home to leftover potatoes and any other vegetables.

For 1

1 tbsp light olive oil
1 banana shallot, finely sliced
75g (2¾oz) cooked new
    potatoes, thickly sliced
2 cloves garlic, 1 crushed, 1 cut
    in half
100g (⅔ cup) tinned flageolet
    beans, drained and rinsed
50g (1¾oz) frozen petit pois

300ml (1¼ cups) chicken or
    vegetable stock
couple of strands of saffron
1 egg
1 thick slice of bread
a clutch of mixed herbs, such
    as mint, parsley and chives
    (optional)
sea salt and black pepper

Heat the olive oil in a small saucepan over a low heat. Add the shallot and a pinch of salt and cook gently for about 7 minutes to soften, stirring regularly. Add the potatoes and crushed garlic and cook for a couple of minutes until the scent of the garlic starts to rise from the pan, then stir, adding a splash more oil if it's all threatening to stick. Now add the stock, saffron and another pinch of salt. When the stock comes to the boil, add the flageolet beans and simmer for 7 minutes before adding the peas. (This would also be the stage to add any other cooked vegetables you might want to use up.) Simmer for another 5 minutes, then taste for seasoning.

Break the egg into a cup or small bowl and carefully slide into the broth. Simmer very gently for about 4 minutes or until the white is set and the yolk is runny.

Meanwhile, toast the bread, then rub the cut side of the remaining garlic clove all over both sides of the toast and sit the garlic toast in a large warm soup bowl.

Carefully lift the egg out of the broth and place on the toast. Stir the herbs into the soup, if using, then ladle the fragrant broth into the bowl.

LAMB AND BARLEY

Pearl barley is one of my go-to comfort ingredients, perhaps because the aroma of cooking barley reminds me of the barley water of my childhood. Every now and again, I still make a batch using the soaking water from barley, and it goes down a storm with one and all. If you're so inclined, set aside the soaking water when you drain the barley; it will keep for a few days in the fridge. Lamb is the obvious pairing with barley, but a vegetarian version with leftover cooked vegetables works just as well – in which case, I might crumble some feta on top.

For 3

200g (1 cup) pearl barley
2 tbsp sunflower or
  grapeseed oil
30g (2 tbsp) butter
1 large leek, washed, trimmed
  and sliced
2 carrots, peeled and cut into
  2-cm (¾-in) chunks
1 small swede (rutabaga),
  peeled and cut into 2-cm
  (¾-in) chunks
2 cloves garlic, crushed

200ml (generous ¾ cup)
  white wine
600ml (2½ cups) vegetable
  stock
250g (9oz) leftover cooked
  lamb, shredded
couple of sprigs of mint,
  chopped
small handful of flat-leaf
  parsley, chopped
sea salt and black pepper

Rinse the barley, then leave to soak for at least 20 minutes.

Heat the oil and half the butter in a large heavy-based saucepan over a medium heat. Add the leek with a pinch of salt and cook gently for about 5 minutes until starting to soften. Add the carrots, swede and garlic and cook for a few minutes, stirring to prevent sticking. Drain the barley and add to the pan. Cook for a minute or so, then add the wine and cook, stirring, until it has been absorbed. Pour in the stock and simmer, stirring from time to time, until the barley is tender. This will take about 30 minutes – top up with hot water if the stock is all absorbed before the barley is soft.

When the barley is nearly done, add the lamb and allow to heat through.

Take the pan off the heat before stirring in the rest of the butter and seasoning with salt and pepper to taste. Leave to sit, covered, for 5 minutes, then stir in the herbs and serve.

PIZZA BY ANY OTHER NAME

What I've done here is turn a pizza on its head: this is basically a slightly sloppier version of the tomato sauce you might spread over a pizza base, spiked with some tasty morsels from the fridge, then topped with mozzarella and chunks of bread and baked. Couldn't be easier, and it needs little in the way of accompaniment – although a green salad is always good. Feel free to pick and choose what to add to the tomato sauce, depending on what leftovers you have.

For 4

3 tbsp extra virgin olive oil
6 rashers streaky bacon
2 red onions, sliced
3 cloves garlic, crushed
2 sprigs of thyme, leaves
    stripped from stems
400g (14oz) stale bread,
    torn into chunks
250g (9oz) mushrooms, sliced

half a 280g (10oz) jar roasted
    red peppers, drained and
    torn into bite-sized pieces
1 x 400g (14oz) tin
    of tomatoes
1 bay leaf
175g (6oz) mozzarella
few sprigs of basil (optional)
sea salt and black pepper

Preheat the oven to 200°C/400°F/gas 6.

Heat a generous splash of olive oil in a large heavy-based saucepan (with a lid) over a medium heat. Using scissors, snip the bacon into chunky lardon-like pieces straight into the hot oil, then let it sizzle and release its fat. As soon as the bacon has browned a little, lift it out with a slotted spoon and set aside. Throw the onions into the pan with a pinch of salt and stir to coat in the bacon fat. Add a splash more oil if they don't look shiny, then turn the heat down to low and cook gently for about 7 minutes, or until soft but not brown.

Meanwhile, make the topping. In a large bowl, mix the garlic and thyme leaves with any remaining olive oil and season with salt and pepper. Throw in the stale bread and toss to coat in the oily mixture. Season generously with black pepper – and maybe a pinch of salt, depending what kind of bread you are using.

When the onions are soft and sweet, turn the heat up to medium and add the mushrooms, along with another sprinkling of salt. Keep the pan moving while the mushrooms cook – this should take about 3–4 minutes. Next, add the peppers, return the bacon and, after a brief stir, add the tomatoes and bay leaf. Bring the lot up to the boil and simmer vigorously for about 5 minutes to let everything get to know each other and for the sauce to reduce a little.

Season with salt and pepper to taste, then pour into a baking dish about 20cm x 15cm (8in x 6in) and shake gently to level, so that it completely covers the base of the dish. Tear the mozzarella – and the basil, if using – into bite-sized pieces and distribute evenly over the tomato sauce. Scatter the bread over the top, making sure everything is covered, then bake in the oven for 15 minutes until golden, crisp and bubbling. Serve straight away.

EPIC BUBBLE AND SQUEAK

Bubble and squeak is such a good place to put all the odds and ends of veg you're left with at the end of the week, making it a classic staff lunch or supper in many restaurants. One particular chef I used to work with, called Paul, is the absolute king of bubble. For me, the trick lies in knowing when to turn the contents of the pan and when to leave them alone to get crisp, and he does this with precision, so that every bubble is a winner. Bubble with fried eggs and bacon is a great plan, but I'd also happily chow down on a plate of bubble and squeak with nothing more than some trusty tomato ketchup. I would counsel sticking with potatoes, root veg and greens when using up leftovers – and if you don't have any remains, just peel and cut some potatoes and veg into chunks and simmer in salted water until cooked. Because this is quite a moveable feast, the quantities very much come down to what you have.

For 2
3 tbsp sunflower or
    grapeseed oil
30g (2 tbsp) butter
½ onion, sliced
250g (9oz) cooked potatoes –
    leftover mash is especially
    good
200g (7oz) cooked root
    vegetables

100g (3½oz) cooked greens,
    roughly chopped – sprouts
    and sprout tops are my
    favourites
sea salt and black pepper
tomato ketchup, mustard
    or sriracha sauce, to serve

Heat the oil and butter in a large heavy-based frying pan over a medium heat. Add the onion, along with a pinch of salt, and let it soften and get a bit of colour for a couple of minutes. Add the potatoes and root veg, flattening them out to cover the whole pan, then leave them alone to get nicely brown and crisp for a good 5 minutes.

At this point, use a fish slice or spatula to lift up a decent chunk of bubble and check if it's brown underneath. If it is, flip it over and squash it down, then do this all over so you get pockets of brown crunchy base nestled into the soft middle part. Keep going with this for a good half an hour, leaving a decent amount of time between each flipping, so the bits on the base get really crisp – I can't emphasize enough what a difference this will make to your bubble and squeak. When you are happy with the amount of crispiness versus softness, stir in the greens and keep stirring and mashing until they are hot.

Spoon onto plates and serve with tomato ketchup, mustard or even sriracha sauce.

DRIPPING ON TOAST WITH CHOPPED BEEF

For the uninitiated, dripping is the fat rendered from beef as it roasts and left behind in the roasting tin. Considered a luxury during wartime rationing, it fell out of fashion for a long time, initially because the idea of leftovers and using every last bit of everything was considered slightly gauche once rationing ended, and later because it was thought to be bad for us. Now, however, dripping has been rehabilitated as it is a very pure form of fat and is considered to be relatively healthy, so long as it is taken in moderation – unless you are swimming the Channel, of course, in which case you can slather it on all over! This recipe is simplicity itself: just toast spread with dripping and then covered with leftover roast beef, watercress and pickled walnuts.

For 1

1 small shallot, finely sliced
2 pickled walnuts, roughly chopped
1 tbsp liquid from the pickled walnut jar
splash of extra virgin olive oil
100g (3½oz) cold roast beef
1 thick slice of bread of
your choice
1 clove garlic, cut in half
15g (1 tbsp) beef dripping, or duck fat or butter
30g (½ cup) watercress, washed and trimmed
sea salt and black pepper

In a small bowl, mix the shallot and pickled walnuts with the liquid from the jar, olive oil and seasoning. Now cut the beef into slices about 3mm (⅛ in) thick, then cut each slice into strips one way and then the other, so you end up with little cubes. Add the beef to the shallot mixture and toss everything together, then check the seasoning.

Meanwhile, toast the bread under a hot grill (broiler), then rub the cut side of the garlic clove over both sides of the toast. Spread one side thickly with dripping, season with salt and pepper and return to the grill until melted.

Pile the chopped beef onto the hot toast and top with watercress. Eat this hot, sweet and salty treat straight away.

Pick-me-ups &
pop-it-in-in-ones

When nothing else will do!

Some Sundays it feels like the only way to get through is with a stiff drink and a little bite to eat. This might be a glass of mulled cider and a plate of delicious cheese with a book on the sofa, or even in bed for the ultimate decadence. Or a hot toddy and a buttered crumpet before a hot bath to chase off a cold. Or a few friends round for some mixology, card games and quick-and-easy mouthfuls of food.

Since the idea is that these will stand in for supper, I have been generous when stating how many each recipe serves – but if you wanted to repurpose any of them as canapés (or pop-it-in-in-ones, as a friend's mum calls them!) for a party, you could probably get away with less per person. I have chosen an edible treat to go with each drink with two little nibbles to spare (quick cheese straws and spiced nuts), which would also be great to go alongside any of the other dishes.

THE DRINKS TROLLEY

Much as I love drinking cocktails, I am no expert, and so I asked friends Harry Darby and Charles Gouldsbrough of the wonderful Gimlet Bar to come up with some simple, uplifting cocktails to suit the joys in this chapter.

'Born out of a piece of performance work at the Slade School of Fine Art, the Gimlet Bar has evolved into a movable cocktail bar-for-hire, serving exquisite drinks made with our own cordials, ferments and infusions. It can be glamorous, but for the most part it means working under some fairly hilarious conditions. We've served drinks in woodland beneath thunderous skies, at a wind-swept lake in the Yorkshire Dales, and even on the prow of a battleship. Although the cocktails below were conceived as playful responses to events or locations – in this case, a film premiere, a period garden and the inauguration of a new arcade machine – we hope they come in handy at home.

Rosie asked us to suggest uncomplicated but delicious drinks that could be made with at least a few of the bottles you're likely to have lying around, so in theory you'll only need to go shopping for a few extras. But if you want to lay in some or all of the following, you can look forward to many hours of happy experimentation.'

Spirits
Brandy, preferably French brandy or cognac
Rye whiskey or bourbon
Gin, preferably London dry
Lillet Blanc, or any sweet white vermouth
Cocchi Americano
Campari
Benedictine
Suze
Pernod, but pastis or ouzo will do

Mixers
Sparkling wine
Simple syrup or, even better, a syrup made with orange
or grapefruit (see page 102)
Elderflower cordial
Tonic water
Soda water, but sparkling mineral water will do

Ice

Some of the recipes call for crushed ice, which cools and dilutes your drink in a very different way from cubed ice – but in the absence of an ice-crusher or powerful blender, ice cubes will do just fine as a substitute.

Cocktail shaker

If you don't have one, you will need to be creative: a screw-top jar or any container with a sturdy lid will do.

Mesh strainer

This removes the finer granules of ice from your drink as you pour it from shaker to glass – these would make your drink watery, with a crunchy texture, which is less enjoyable. If you don't have one, try using a kitchen sieve instead.

A note on measurements

We've given the measurements as parts (or ratios), so you can scale your drinks up or down as the occasion or size of vessel demands. Beware, though – all spirits have their own unique flavour, so we recommend you *always* taste your mixture before shaking that cocktail! You may also prefer a less 'pokey' drink than we do.

SIMPLE SYRUP
for better-tasting cocktails, the Gimlet Bar way

There are lots of ways to make a sugar syrup. As a general rule our syrups are made without any cooking. We find this produces a fresher and more delicate flavour, and provided you have enough time to let the mixture infuse, it's actually simpler to make.

Zest your fruit of choice into a bowl. The cocktails here call for orange or grapefruit, but in theory any fruit, herb or edible flower will make a tasty drink.

Chop and juice the 'zested' fruit (if you're making a herb or flower syrup, you'll need to use water in place of citrus juice – add enough to cover your ingredients). Add to the bowl, along with enough sugar to give a syrupy consistency, roughly a 1:1 ratio, stirring until the sugar has completely dissolved – this can take a bit of time. If you've added too much sugar by accident and your syrup has become stiff, mix in enough water to loosen it up.

Leave the mixture to infuse in a refrigerator – 24 hours is best.

Taste it – a syrup should by nature be sweet, as when used in a cocktail it will be combined with citrus juice and alcohol; however, a little lemon juice added at this stage can help to 'brighten' the flavour of your chosen ingredients.

Strain through a sieve and bottle, then store in the refrigerator.

Your syrup will stay fresh for around one month, after which point a slight 'fizz' may develop. Fear not – a lightly sparkling syrup is a sign that fermentation is under way, a guarantee against your mixture ever spoiling. Happily enough, you now also have a slightly alcoholic syrup with arguably more interesting flavours! In fact, we use many fermented syrups in our cocktails.

LIGHT-EMITTING DIODE

This variant of a whiskey sour almost glows in the dark, perhaps due to the opalescent Pernod and the silky frothed egg white. It will relieve any excesses of dinner and have you jumping around in no time. At any rate, it's more invigorating than licking an AA battery. A perfect partner to the squash and truffle brandade overleaf.

1 part rye whiskey or bourbon
⅓ part simple syrup, ideally
infused with orange or grapefruit zest
⅓ part lemon juice
dash of Pernod – or pastis or ouzo,
if that's all you can get your hands on
2 tsp egg white
ice cubes
frond of fennel or dill

Combine the whiskey, syrup, lemon juice, Pernod and egg white in a shaker, or a jar with a lid and add plenty of ice.

Shake vigorously until well chilled and the egg white is foaming.

Strain into a cocktail glass, ideally a stemmed one, using a mesh strainer or sieve – you may wish to spoon some of the egg-white foam from the shaker onto your drink if too much gets left behind.

Delicately garnish with a frond of fennel or dill – a little bit of green foliage sitting atop the frothy head of this drink is most appealing.

Sip and perform a backwards somersault.

SQUASH AND TRUFFLE BRANDADE

Strictly speaking, *brandade* is a Provençal dish of salt cod puréed with garlic, olive oil and sometimes potato, but I have used it in this context because the texture of the end result is similar. We're so spoilt these days with the wide range of squash and pumpkins available to us. In their many guises, they make such a wonderful autumnal treat and I tend to cook with them as much as I can during their season. They keep brilliantly, too, so can brighten up the long winter months of roots and brassicas. The varieties I really rate are Crown Prince, which can be quite big but keep very well; and Cream of the Crop is a nice little one, as is the gem squash. Another favourite is spaghetti squash, which I think works particularly well in this recipe. Some squashes can be quite watery, so I tend to capture that liquid and reduce it down and add it back to the squash. If you are lucky enough to lay your hands on a truffle, then shave it on top, but good-quality truffle oil does the trick, too. If you're feeling extra-decadent, you can grate over a little cheese as well – parmesan would be my recommendation.

For 6

1 small squash, about 680g (1½lb)
2 tsp olive oil
small grating of nutmeg
60g (4 tbsp) unsalted butter

1 tbsp truffle oil
3 pitta breads or flatbreads
a few shavings of fresh truffle (optional)
sea salt and black pepper

Preheat the oven to 180°C/350°F/gas 4.

Cut the squash in half and scrape out the seeds with a spoon. Season the flesh side liberally with salt and pepper, then grate over a little nutmeg. Put each half onto a large sheet of oiled foil, skin side down, then splash over the rest of the olive oil and a good smattering of water. Wrap up the squash to form two parcels and bake for 50–60 minutes or until totally soft but not brown. Scrape all the flesh out and if it seems rather waterlogged, tip the lot into a sieve set over a saucepan and let the liquid drip through for about half an hour, or until the squash looks dry. Then put the pan over a medium heat and let the liquid simmer and reduce until syrupy.

Meanwhile, mash the squash. When the liquid has reduced, add the squash to the pan to warm through. Now gradually beat in the butter, bit by bit, until you have a lovely rich and glossy mixture. Season to taste with salt and pepper, then stir in three-quarters of the truffle oil.

Put the pitta breads or flatbreads under a hot grill (broiler) to warm through, then cut into bite-sized strips.

Scrape the squash *brandade* into a warm bowl and sprinkle with the rest of the truffle oil (now is the time for a few shavings of truffle, if you have one tucked away somewhere!), then surround with the strips of bread.

REICHENBACH FALLS

Our English hero Sherlock Holmes (the London dry gin) sets out to the Alps (the fresh Lillet) to battle his nemesis Moriarty at a famous waterfall; with spray on their faces, they plunge to the rocks below (the earthy tone of gentian root in Suze). This 'white negroni' uses Lillet, with its pronounced citrus notes, instead of sweet vermouth, and Suze rather than Campari as the bitter element.

1 part Suze
1 part London dry gin
1 part Lillet Blanc or any sweet white vermouth
dash of lemon juice
ice cubes
lemon slices

Pour the Suze, gin, Lillet and lemon juice into a small tumbler or 'rocks' glass half-filled with ice and stir well.

Top up with more ice and garnish with several half-moon-shaped slices of lemon.

Beware – this is a strong drink. We like to leave it to cool and come together in the glass for a minute or two before drinking. If it's still too strong for your taste, a dash of soda or sparkling water is the answer.

SHALLOT, PARMESAN AND OLIVE TOASTS

This recipe comes from my time working for the truly great Shaun Hill at his Merchant House restaurant in Ludlow, where these toasts were served as a treat on arrival – a fantastic mixture of strong flavours to pack a punch with a bracing drink. My father was an avid tomato peeler, and I have followed his lead in cooked dishes; the only time I don't worry so much is if they are tiny little ones, then I live and let live. This recipe also requires some fairly high-level chopping, as you want a very small dice to make a canapé-sized toast-topper, but the result is definitely worth it. Just make sure you have a sharp knife to make the task bearable.

For 6

5 large tomatoes, peeled, deseeded and finely diced

2 small banana shallots, finely diced

2 small cloves garlic, crushed

100ml (7 tbsp) extra virgin olive oil

80g (⅔ cup) stone-in black olives – the very best you can find

50g (⅓ cup) anchovy-stuffed green olives

25g (⅓ cup) coarsely grated pecorino

small handful of flat-leaf parsley, finely chopped

1 good-quality baguette, sliced

sea salt and black pepper

Put the tomatoes, shallots, garlic and olive oil into a bowl. Give everything a good stir, so the flavours can get to know each other while you take on the slightly laborious task of pitting the black olives or cutting the flesh from around the pit. Finely dice both the black and green olives and add to the bowl, along with the pecorino and parsley. Taste and season with salt and pepper accordingly.

Grill the slices of baguette, cutting them in half if they're too big for a mouthful, and spoon over any juices that have come out of the olive mixture. Pile on a generous spoonful of the mixture and serve straight away.

WHAT THE DICKENS?!

Good grief! Brandy and tonic water? What the Dickens?! We created this sweet medicinal drink for Mr Ralph Fiennes, to celebrate his historical film masterpiece *The Invisible Woman* – it will fulfil your Great Expectations, even in Hard Times or in the Bleakest House…

crushed ice
1 part French brandy or cognac
1 part Benedictine
¼ part lemon juice
2 parts tonic water
thickly pared strip of lemon zest
paper drinking straw

Half-fill a small metal Julep cup, 'rocks' glass or short tumbler with ice.

Pour in the brandy, Benedictine, lemon juice and tonic water and stir well.

Top up your glass with plenty of ice.

Twist the strip of lemon zest over the drink to release the lemon oil, then tuck it into the ice and add a straw.

CROUTE WINDSOR

When I worked for Tim Hayward at the Cambridge institution that is Fitzbillies, he introduced me to a splendid recipe book by Robin McDouall called *Clubland Cooking*, which chimed with the old-school baked goods fondly recalled by some of the veteran bakers at Fitzbillies. Like many recipes of their era, most contain lashings of cream, truffles, caviar or brandy, but I love their simplicity. Croute Windsor is based on a savoury from a London club called White's, although sadly there's no explanation of how it got its name.

For 1

generous splash of light olive oil
1 flat mushroom, peeled and
    thickly sliced
50g (1¾oz) best-quality ham,
    thickly sliced if possible
clutch of chives
a splash of sherry or a squeeze

of lemon juice
2 tbsp crème fraîche
1 slice of bread – to give this
    the decadence it's craving,
    I'd go for brioche
sea salt and black pepper

Heat the olive oil in a small frying pan over a medium heat. Add the mushroom with a pinch of salt and let it cook down until soft.

Meanwhile, cut the ham into long ribbons about 2cm (¾in) wide and chop the chives.

Add the ham to the mushrooms and let it warm through. Gently simmer away any excess liquid, then add the splash of sherry or squeeze of lemon. Once this has reduced to almost nothing, stir in the crème fraîche and simmer until the sauce is coating everything nicely. Season with salt and pepper to taste, then throw in the chives.

Leave to tick away gently while you toast the bread, then pile this marvellous mixture on top.

TERRAZZO

A veritable palate-cleanser: crisp, cooling like marble, almost flinty and savoury. Decorated with diced lime, lemon, orange and a zigzag of bay leaf to create a jazzy terrazzo effect, this fizzy aperitivo uses Cocchi Americano, a bitter Italian aperitif wine with citrus and herbal flavours – making it the perfect start to any bunga bunga party…

crushed ice
small segments of lime, lemon, orange
½ part gin
1 part Cocchi Americano
2 parts sparkling wine
paper drinking straw
bay leaf

Half fill a highball or other tall glass with ice, adding small segments of lime, lemon and orange as you go to mimic terrazzo.

Pour in the gin, Cocchi Americano and sparkling wine and stir well.

Top up with more ice and citrus segments.

Add a straw and finish your drink with a bay leaf garnish, decoratively cut with a pair of scissors to a design of your choice – we normally go for a zig-zag.

ANCHOVY-STUFFED EGGS

A fabulous throwback dish of such ease and unassuming style, stuffed eggs give immense amounts of pleasure. My dear friend Peter and I once met in a bar in Manhattan to drink martinis and share a couple of plates of their famous devilled eggs, bringing to mind this quote from Pulitzer-prize-winning journalist Herb Caen: 'Martinis are like breasts, one isn't enough and three is too many'. In my book, it's a sentiment that applies equally to stuffed eggs. The most delicious stuffed eggs I have eaten in recent memory – and the inspiration for this recipe – were at a supper cooked by the amazing James Ferguson, a dream of a chef.

For 1

2 eggs
20g (2 tbsp) anchovies,
    quite finely chopped
1 tsp olive oil
finely grated zest and juice
    of ¼ lemon
½ tsp Dijon mustard

generous pinch of smoked
    paprika
2 tbsp mayonnaise
small handful of parsley,
    finely chopped
cornichons or small pickled
    onions, to serve

Put the eggs into a saucepan of cold water and bring to the boil, then turn down the heat so the water is just ticking over and leave to cook for 12 minutes.

Meanwhile, put the anchovies into a bowl with the oil and mash to a paste, then add the lemon zest, mustard, paprika and mayonnaise and mix until smooth. Stir in the parsley.

By now the eggs should be ready to be lifted out and run under cold water until completely cold – this will take a good few minutes.

Carefully peel the eggs and cut them in half lengthways. Scoop out the yolks and add to the anchovy mixture, then mash lightly together – I like a little bit of texture. Taste the stuffing mixture, then add some of the lemon juice and season with salt and pepper.

Depending on how many cocktails you are planning to have, it might be worth taking a tiny slice from the bottom of each egg white 'boat' so they sit steady on the plate. Spoon or, if you're feeling super-fancy, pipe the stuffing back into the egg white boats, then serve at room temperature with a few cornichons or little pickled onions.

WOOLF

This is a real snuggler – a fireside drink for the Bloomsbury set. Curl up with a good book after dinner and this spiced, creamy drink as the ideal companion.

ice cubes
1 part Benedictine
2 parts whole (full-fat) milk
orange slices
freshly grated nutmeg

Half-fill a small tumbler or 'rocks' glass with ice.

Combine the Benedictine and milk in a shaker, or a jar with a lid, and add plenty of ice.

Shake vigorously until well chilled and the milk is frothing, then strain into the glass using a mesh strainer or sieve.

Top up your drink with an extra ice cube (or two) and decorate with half-moon-shaped slices of orange and a generous grating of nutmeg.

DEVILS ON HORSEBACK

I have very early memories of this sweet and salty treat. My parents always had a party on Christmas Eve, complete with handbell ringers, and every year we would spend the whole day making tasty little morsels to pass around. Devils on horseback always passed muster, whereas vol au vents with many a filling came and went, along with the seventies. Stuffed mushrooms, mangetouts and all things minimal blew away with the eighties. By the nineties, when interest from the rest of the family had waned, I pressed on with many an ambitious snackette, but always with a trusty prune wrapped in bacon by my side. Such a comfort. I have, on occasion, speared them with a (de-leafed) rosemary or thyme stalk for extra aromatic depth, but if life feels too short for such things, just strew some herbs over the bottom of the baking tray. These make perfect party food: the amounts below are easy enough to multiply up if feeding a crowd; and, once they're wrapped in bacon, your devils on horseback will happily sit in the fridge until you're ready to pop them into the oven.

For 2

6 rashers of smoked
    streaky bacon
12 soft prunes
2 tsp extra virgin olive oil

rosemary, thyme and bay
    leaves (optional)
black pepper
bread, to serve

Preheat the oven to 190°C/375°F/gas 5.

Cut the bacon rashers in half and stretch slightly by pressing along them with the back of a knife.

Put the prunes into a bowl with the oil and a grinding of pepper, and toss to make sure they are well coated. Roll each prune in half a rasher of bacon and sit on a baking tray (strewn with rosemary, thyme and bay, if you fancy), seam side down, and in a single layer but not touching.

Cook your devils on horseback in the oven for about 15–20 minutes, by which time you will have crisp bacon, unctuous prunes and tasty juices for mopping up with bread.

TRAINWRECK

This will either cause an incident or revive those at the scene. For this drink, crushed ice is best, as it helps to cool the ingredients quickly and melts in such a way as to soften the harshness of the alcohol. But if you don't have an ice-crusher or a powerful blender, ice cubes will do.

crushed ice
1 part rye whiskey or bourbon
½ part Campari
½ part simple syrup, ideally infused with orange or grapefruit zest
1 part orange juice – or, if in season, blood orange juice
orange slices, for decoration
paper drinking straw

Half-fill a small metal Julep cup, 'rocks' glass or short tumbler with ice.

Pour in the rye whiskey or bourbon, Campari, simple syrup and orange juice and stir well.

Top up with enough ice to give your drink a bountiful appearance.

Garnish with half-moon-shaped slices of orange and add a straw.

WHITE BEAN CROQUETTES WITH HERBY MAYONNAISE

A few stints of living in the south of Spain have made me a big croquette aficionado. I particularly like this type for home cooking because it doesn't involve making a bechamel sauce, and so is relatively simple and very tasty. All in all, a good robust option for a Sunday night.

For 4 (makes 8)

1 tbsp extra virgin olive oil
1 medium red onion,
*   finely sliced*
1 small sprig rosemary, leaves
*   stripped and finely chopped*
2 cloves garlic, crushed
120g (2 ⅓ cups)
*   baby spinach leaves*
1 x 400g (14oz) tin of
*   cannellini beans, drained*

100g (1½ cups) panko or
*   other breadcrumbs*
1 tbsp finely chopped mint
1 tbsp finely chopped parsley
generous pinch of chilli flakes
75g (⅓ cup) mayonnaise
1 egg
6 tbsp light olive oil

Heat the extra virgin olive oil in a saucepan over a low heat and add the onion and rosemary. Cook very gently until soft and sweet, then add the garlic and stir about for a minute. Add the spinach and mix thoroughly, stirring until it wilts down. Once completely wilted and soft, add the beans and warm through.

Transfer the contents of the pan to a food processor and whizz to a smooth paste. Add 20g (⅓ cup) breadcrumbs and pulse to combine. The mixture should be quite stiff – if it seems too wet, add some more breadcrumbs. Scrape into a bowl and transfer to the fridge for an hour or so. Meanwhile, stir the mint, parsley and chilli flakes into the mayonnaise.

Crack the egg into a shallow bowl and beat lightly. Put the breadcrumbs into another shallow bowl. Scoop out tablespoonfuls of the chilled croquette mixture, roll into balls and then flatten into little pucks. Dip the croquettes in beaten egg and then breadcrumbs, shaking off any excess. If I have time, I like to double-dip the croquettes to give them an extra-crispy shell.

Heat the light olive oil in a small frying pan and, when the oil is good and hot, fry the croquettes in batches of three so you don't lower the temperature of the oil too much. Keep turning them until they are golden all over, then drain on kitchen paper. Eat while hot, dipped in, or drizzled with, the herby mayo.

GARDENERS' QUESTION TIME

The bright floral notes and refreshing green hint of cucumber in this drink are as fragrant as reclining on a recently mown lawn. This simple yet elegant sour can be consumed at any time of day but is particularly excellent for a garden party. Just remember to plan ahead, so you have time to infuse the gin with cucumber overnight. It is a joyous pairing with both the chicory leaves opposite, and the smoked mackerel dip on page 118.

1 part gin, infused with slices of cucumber for up to 24 hours
⅓ part elderflower cordial
⅓ part lemon juice
ice cubes
cluster of elderflowers or a slice of cucumber

Combine the gin, cordial and lemon juice in a shaker, or a jar with a lid, and add plenty of ice.

Shake vigorously until well chilled.

Strain into a cocktail glass, ideally a stemmed one, using a mesh strainer or sieve.

Mount a generous cluster of elderflowers or a slice of cucumber on the rim of your glass.

PEAR, WALNUT AND STICHELTON INSIDE A CHICORY LEAF

Always quite nice to have something a little bit crunchy and healthy to go with a drink. This is a classic salad in a portable, pop-it-in style-y. Stichelton is a wonderful cheese made at the Welbeck Estate in Nottinghamshire by Joe Schneider using raw milk and natural rennet, and its flavours have a lot in common with Stilton – hence the name, which is said to be the 13th-century name for the village of Stilton. If you can't get hold of Stichelton, feel free to use a good-quality Stilton.

For 6

2 heads of chicory (Belgian endive)	1 tbsp sherry vinegar
	3 tbsp olive oil
50g (½ cup) walnut halves	90g (3oz) Stichelton
2 pears	sea salt and black pepper

Preheat the oven to 180°C/350°F/gas 4.

Carefully separate the leaves of the chicory, discarding any bruised outer ones; some of the bigger leaves may be a little over-sized for this dainty little number, so I tend to save those for a green salad. Finely slice any middling ones and put in a bowl, ready to go inside the leaves with the pear and walnut mix. Arrange the smaller chicory leaves on a plate.

Spread out the walnuts on a baking tray and toast in the oven for 5–6 minutes until golden. Remove from the oven and, while the walnuts are still warm, give them a gentle rub in kitchen paper or a clean tea towel to get rid of any loose skin, then chop them roughly and add to the bowl of sliced chicory. Peel and core the pears and cut them into bite-sized pieces and add to bowl as well.

Dress with the sherry vinegar and olive oil, then crumble in the Stichelton and mix everything together. Season to taste with salt and pepper, then spoon the filling into the leaves and serve straight away.

SMOKED MACKEREL
AND HORSERADISH DIP
WITH CRUDITÉS

Smoked mackerel has an enduring appeal. And, although dips often get left behind at parties for the razzle-dazzle of pastry items, at the end of the night you will find people diving in! Essentially, this is a cross between a loose paté and a dip, which makes it very versatile. As far as crudités are concerned, I favour fennel, radishes, carrots and cucumber – and actually I love a Bath Oliver or other ship's biscuit for dipping.

For 2

175g (6oz) smoked
   mackerel fillets
30g (2 tbsp) soft butter
1 tbsp creamed horseradish
few sprigs of tarragon, leaves
   picked and roughly chopped

finely grated zest and juice
   of ½ lemon
60ml (¼ cup) crème fraîche
raw vegetables of your choice,
   for dipping

Take the skin off the mackerel and break up the fish, checking for bones as you go. Put it in a food processor, along with the butter, horseradish, tarragon and lemon zest, and whizz to a smooth paste. Now add the crème fraîche and a squeeze of lemon juice.

Process for a little longer until the dip is light and fluffy with a nice scoop-able consistency, then taste and season with salt, pepper and lemon juice accordingly. Scrape into a bowl and serve with your choice of crudités for dipping.

SPICED NUTS

A handful of nuts with a good strong drink is a real livener. I make these nuts quite regularly at home and they often appear as a bar snack in establishments where I'm involved with the menu because they go down a treat. Don't be tempted to taste the glaze before you put it on the nuts as it will be very strong at that stage – it took me a while when I was developing this recipe to realise quite how much flavour the nuts suck up. A bit of finely chopped rosemary is a nice addition. Any leftover spiced nuts will keep in an airtight container for a week or so.

For 6

1 large egg white	3 tsp cayenne pepper
75g (⅓ cup) light brown soft sugar	100g (¾ cup) peanuts
	60g (½ cup) cashews
3 tsp celery salt	60g (½ cup) almonds
2¼ tsp chilli flakes	60g (½ cup) brazils
1½ tsp ground allspice	60g (⅔ cup) pecans
2¼ tsp ground cumin	50g (⅓ cup) pumpkin seeds

Preheat the oven to 180°C/350°F/gas 4 and line a large baking tray with baking paper.

Whisk the egg white to stiff peaks, then fold in the sugar, salt and spices. Stir in the nuts and mix to coat well then spread out the nuts in a single layer on the baking tray. Cook the nuts in the oven for 10 minutes, then stir to separate them a little and turn the oven down to 160°C/325°F/gas 3 and cook for another 10 minutes. When they're ready, the nuts should be light golden with a darker coating. Remove from the oven and stir again to break up any lumps, then leave to cool and get crisp, stirring from time to time – they may well stick together as they cool, but you should be able to break them up pretty easily.

QUICK CHEESE STRAWS

My first job as a chef was at the iconic Carved Angel in Dartmouth, working for the wonderful Joyce Molyneux. She has been the biggest inspiration throughout my cooking life, and continues to be: I still visit her a couple of times a year, and she will always have made a biscuit or something for us to have with our tea. At the Carved Angel, we served cheese straws and olives on arrival, and so one of the first jobs we learned was to make and roll endless numbers of the things, but they were so melt-in-the-mouth we soon forgave them their monotonous toil. I regularly make these quick ones with any pastry off-cuts, shortcrust or puff – or buy ready-rolled for extra ease, and to allow time to make some cocktails to go alongside! I use a dry-ish cheese like parmesan, because it packs more of a flavour punch, but do experiment. Ditto with the seeds that go on top: cumin adds a note of warm spiciness; caraway and onion a kind of sweet musky appeal; celery and dill a herby mellowness. Sesame and poppy are a constant, as they add texture and carry the other flavours. As these cheese straws freeze very well, making a bigger batch seems sensible…

Makes about 32 straws

400g (14oz) shortcrust
    or puff pastry
flour, for dusting
1 scant tbsp Dijon mustard
80g (1¼ cups) freshly grated
    parmesan

1 egg, lightly beaten
generous pinch each of
    poppy and sesame seeds,
    plus your choice of cumin,
    caraway, onion, celery and
    dill seeds

Preheat the oven to 200°C/400°F/gas 6 and line a large baking sheet with baking paper.

Dust your work surface with a little flour and roll out the pastry to a 1.5mm (1/16in) thickness, or just lay it out if it is already rolled.

Paint the whole sheet of pastry with the mustard and scatter all but a tablespoon of the parmesan on top. Fold the pastry in half and then roll it out again to double its length, so it's 3mm (1/8in) thick.

Paint the whole lot with beaten egg, then cut into 1cm (1/2in) wide strips. Arrange side by side on the baking sheet and sprinkle over the seeds – I prefer to concentrate the seeds around the middle of the straws as I think they look good like that. Scatter over the remaining cheese and bake for 10–12 minutes until crisp and golden. Eat as soon as cooled!

INDEX

ACKNOWLEDGEMENTS
AND THANK YOU'S

I would like to thank everyone listed below:

The idea for this book came from the inspired and very generous Ed Griffiths
– his confidence in my ability to breathe life into his idea was unerring.

Luckily the wonderful Sarah Lavelle saw the beauty in the idea too,
found the perfect tone and style for it and put together a fabulous team
to work on the book, namely:

Helen Lewis, the calm and super-stylish creative director.
Alison Cowan, a great editor who understood my style immediately
and made the whole process very easy.
Patricia Niven, a good friend and truly inspiring photographer, and her
super-efficient assistant Jessica, who also got all my IT sorted out!!
Will Webb, our masterly book designer.
Rosie Reynolds, who cooked and styled the food with such ease and grace,
and Nena Foster who assisted and cooked up a storm.
Rachel Vere, who found all the right props and set the tone so well.
Also Dan and Joana at Penn Street studios not least for tolerating
Florence the sausage dog.

My agent and dear friend Victoria Hobbs, who has such great trust in my
abilities and gave me the confidence just to go for it.

Harry Darby and Charles Gouldsbrough of the Gimlet Bar (www.gimlet-bar.
com), with whom I have spent many, many a happy hour – they have laid on a
superb raft of Sunday night shakers and movers for the final chapter.

Alexis Snell, the creator of the beautiful cover and motifs throughout the book
– the most talented artist and lovely pen pal one could wish for.

All the women in the food world who have supported, guided and/or inspired
me over the years, most of whom I am also lucky to count as great friends:
Joyce Molyneux, Leila McAlister, Polly Russell, Laura Jackson, Lori de Mori,
Claire Roberson, Kitty Travers, Rachel Roddy, Anna Tobias, Margot Hender-
son, Pauline Griffiths, Angela Hartnett, Laura Hearn, Emma Miles, Rachel
O'Sullivan, Juliet Peston, Sue Lewis, Roisin Hendron, Mady Espirito Santo.

The same goes for these chaps:
Shaun Hill, Adam Sellar, Stevie Williams, Fergus Henderson, Karl Goward, Tim Dillon, James Ferguson, Kevin McFadden, Jack Van Praag, Leo Riethoff, Jacques Espirito Santo, Duncan Catchpole.

My dear friends old and new – this has a big overlap with the above – you all know who you are!
Imogen Loke, Thomas Blythe, Bob Granleese, my sisters Annabel and Camilla and their families, Aunty Mary, Aunty Caroline, Sarah Hammond, Charley McKie-Riethoff, Emily Heath, William Griffiths, Sarah Winman, Rob Bradshaw, Peter Giddens, Sam Walker, Chloe Gartenmann, Jude Sanders, Gillian Ivory, Emma Brook, Ana Garcia and her wonderful family especially Patricia, Reyes and Isabel, Antonio Marin and all my Granadinos, Andrew St Clair, Ben Llewelyn, all my pals past and present of Pint Shop, especially George Perry for his wordsmithery.

Little Florence Salome, my darling wire-haired miniature dachshund, who keeps me grounded and makes me and the majority of people smile endlessly.

My big, strong sister Annabel needs an extra-special mention for being so unconditional in her love and support of me through a couple of pretty hideous years.

My mother is the reason I cook – we baked a lot when I was a kid and I took over a lot of cooking duties in my teens, and for this I am eternally grateful. Not everybody has a job that is also a vocation and a love.

Finally those who are gone and sorely missed:

My father, who was a kind, gentle and clever man and always found time to enjoy cooking and talking about food with me.

My brother Chris, a beautiful and sensitive soul who was a great friend and with whom I spent many a happy hour in the kitchen.

My cousin Sarah, who brought so much joy into our French house over the past few summers.